The Simpler Life

Deborah DeFord

The Simpler Life

An Inspirational Guide to
Living Better with Less

Deborah DeFord

 Reader's Digest

The Reader's Digest Association, Inc.
Pleasantville, NY/Montreal

Acknowledgments

With thanks to Reader's Digest Trade Books Executive Editor, Joseph Gonzalez, and Senior Design Director, Henrietta Stern, for their skill, sensitivity, and patient involvement in the making of this book. And to Ron DeFord, for his willing and discerning ear each step of the way.

A **Reader's Digest Simpler Life**™ Book

Produced by *Frontline Associates,* West Boylston, MA
Producers *Deborah DeFord* and *Michele Italiano-Perla*
Design by *Michele Italiano-Perla*
Illustrations by *Linda Frichtel*

Library of Congress Cataloging in Publication Data
DeFord, Deborah H.
     The Simpler Life : an inspirational guide to living better with
  less / Deborah DeFord.
          p.   cm.
     Includes bibliographical references.
     ISBN 0-7621-0061-3
     1. Conduct of life.   2. Simplicity.   I. Title.
BJ1496.D44   1998
646.7—dc21   97-46151

Printed in the United States of America

This book is dedicated to my parents, Henry and Betty Hellyer,

who showed me what it means to live each day

with grace and gratitude.

Contents

This is a book about the good life that money won't buy. It grew out of my own experience and the experience of others who, in one way or another, discovered that we weren't living the life we want to live. Although many of us had enough and more in material terms, we came up short on the happiness scale. Our lives were too complicated, too busy and stressful. We needed a fresh look at how we'd gotten to this less-than-satisfying existence and how we could make it better. The following pages offer a glimpse of the alternatives some of us have found.

This is a book about possibilities. We all come equipped with a unique set of abilities and passions, backgrounds and potentials. How we build on the basic equipment helps to set the course of our lives. But the course is never set in concrete. We can always reroute along the way if we find that the way is not taking us where we want to go. The chapters that follow give some practical words on the choices open to every one of us as we consider new directions.

This is also a book about balance. Life offers us each an ever-changing mix of givens and choices. We may wish for a simpler life that is a quick fix away — something we can achieve in three easy steps or five simple lessons or through some other formula. But in reality, the simpler life that offers authentic satisfaction and meaning does not come in a package. It is created from within ourselves daily, as we recognize and weigh the alternatives life is affording us day by day. We measure our choices against the counterweights of our deepest values and most cherished dreams, learning in the process what to let go, what to hold onto and where to go next. The pages ahead present a heart-centered perspective on finding the dreams behind our wishes and realistically devising a life that fulfills them.

Don't think of this as a book of answers or solutions. Think of it as a conversation among friends who are looking for a simpler, better way. Take it in small doses or swallow it in a single gulp. Come back to it and consider what it has to offer you today. Question its assumptions and let it challenge yours, just as the best of discussions always do.

D.D., May 1998

Simply Yourself

We read about it in the "Living" section of the Sunday paper. Joe and Mary

Somebody, lately of Big City, Anywhere, have taken a footpath off the fast lane of

modern life. "From high-rise to homestead," the headline reads, accompanied by

photographs of a phone-free log cabin, smiling tanned faces and a long view of the

mountains. Something in us sighs. How did they do it? we ask. These folks have

discovered something about life and what makes it good. Even more, perhaps,

they've discovered something about themselves.

As far as I know, no one has ever isolated a human gene that predisposes us to complicate our lives. Joe and Mary may have hit the "tilt" button at some dramatic and memorable moment in their life together, but they built up to that point by degrees, over time, decision by decision. They weren't born there.

In fact, life is pretty simple at birth. We need food, sleep, shelter and cuddling, and that's about all that we demand. The rest accumulates over time. And as we approach the twenty-first century, "the rest" is nearly beyond imagining.

It wasn't until I got serious about simplifying my life that I began to realize how well trained I am in the art of complicating it. I learned early — in school, in the shopping mall and in front of the television — to have a lot, do a lot, expect a lot and lug a lot around with me from one place and phase of life to another. Now I'm all grown up, and year by year I've added to both my busyness and my belongings. And I'm not alone. Conversations with dozens of others about their lives have convinced me that I'm in good company. The trouble is, it doesn't seem to be making us happy.

I recently heard a speaker addressing what he saw as the most pressing need among the people of his audience. "Too much of a good thing," he proclaimed. "We're overwhelmed and underfulfilled. 'Too much' has become endemic in our society."

Endemic means "characteristic" or "pervasive." I think *epidemic* — that is, excessively pervasive and, what's more, contagious — may be closer to the mark. In fact, we of the industrialized, technologized Western world can hardly imagine a simpler life anymore. We live in a time of unprecedented consumption and a seemingly endless supply of opportunities. We are bombarded daily with more information from all over the world than was even dreamed of as few as ten years ago. We can travel to the other side of our globe in less than 24 hours. Thanks to satellites, phone, fax and the Internet, we can communicate instantly with people virtually anywhere (including outer space), buy and sell goods, engage in high finance, handle personal funds, and order a dinner without leaving our homes.

Not only is all of this available (for a price, of course), but some of the most creative talents in our workforce today dedicate the best years of their lives to designing the advertisements that will convince us that we need all of the above. No wonder that so many of us feel overwhelmed.

We might be tempted to say that a simpler life in today's world is the stuff of movies and fairy tales. Joe and Mary, in their mountainside cabin, are either oddballs, independently wealthy or actors in an enticing promotion campaign for some super-vehicle with all-wheel drive and the ultimate in suspension.

But Joe and Mary are not a myth. They are part of a growing population of people who are committed to taking charge of their lives and carving something simpler, more meaningful and joyful out of them.

Creating simplicity in the complex world in which we live requires an active effort, of course. A simpler life will not just happen. Modern society, while offering an endless supply of products and possibilities "guaranteed" to make our lives easier, rarely suggests and virtually never supports a life that is simpler. Easy and simple are not the same.

We need to begin by asking what constitutes a simple life. For Joe and Mary — who, it turns out, left a costly uptown apartment and high-power positions with a prestigious investment firm — their hands-on, slow-paced organic style of life has eliminated much of what robbed them of happiness and a sense of fulfillment. For Mary's father, on the other hand, a weeklong visit with the couple was a peculiar sort of torture. "Give me my daily newspaper, the corner delicatessen and a good game of golf," he says. "*That's* simple!"

Clearly one person's passion can be another's poison. Simpler living is a quality of life that is coaxed out of chaos and complexity one person at a time. We each have to seek and shape it, consciously and conscientiously. The simpler life will be simpler only as it takes the shape that is appropriate to our individual values, tastes, goals and dispositions. This is where we begin and where we will return, again and again.

I've embarked on the adventure of creating a simpler life for myself. I've had to start with who I am, what I believe in and what I hope for. You have to start with you.

When we arrive on the scene, we're helpless creatures with focused needs and simple satisfactions. By the time we're adults, we've been at the complication game for so long that we often come to view all the extras and accretions of modern life as necessities. It takes a spirit of restored innocence and an act of will to revisit the possibility of simplicity.

Specifically, it takes two fundamental qualities — two "I" strands in the fabric of the life we're examining — to bring us back to simplicity: *integrity* and *intentionality*. Integrity has to do with who we are and what is essential to us. Intentionality refers to what we do, not by instinct or accident but on purpose. Being and doing are the fundamental materials of human existence: if we want to change the character of our life, to make it more satisfying and richer, we have to concentrate on these materials. It is here that we find our own way to turn complicated, clumsy, even regretted lives into simple works of beauty.

Integrity: Getting back to the real me

The dictionary defines *integrity* as "the quality or state of being complete or undivided." In other words, integrity equals wholeness; in practical terms, what shows on the outside matches what exists on the inside; action reflects attitudes and attributes.

What would happen to your life today if you could eliminate everything from it that didn't ring "true" to who you are and to your deepest convictions and loves?

Transforming your life in such a way depends on a critical first step: you need to know, or remember, who you are. What do you value? What or whom do you obey? What principles form the foundation on which you build your life? For many of us, the answers to these questions have become more than a little fuzzy. We have accepted other people's valuations and expectations of us to such an extent that we've lost sight of our own self-perception. Or we never consciously formed one in the first place. Or we've lived so busy a life for so long that the big picture is long lost in a series of fast decisions, spontaneous reactions and hasty accommodations. We have bought too many messages of highly skilled advertisers and have fallen for the latest definition of the "successful" or "sexy" or "happy" person. One way or another, we need to find our way to that big picture — whether it's a return or a new adventure — that ought to frame our lives.

TO KNOW YOURSELF

Create your own space. Uncover what matters to you.

How do you get back to the real you? You will only find your way if you make room for the search and then put yourself to the effort. Many a dream has gone unrealized for no better reason than inattention and inaction.

Create your own space.

First of all — and there's no getting around this — *we have to slow down and create some individual space.*

I interrupted a recent spell of busyness to travel to my second daughter's home. She was due to have surgery, and she needed someone to come and take care of her during her recovery. It was a tough time for me to get away, but I was needed.

My daughter lives six hours away from me, by car or by train. I could have driven and taken work with me. Instead I took the train and left most of the work on my desk. As the locomotive pulled out of the station, I felt a great relief at leaving the work and home demands behind me, even if for only four days. In the many hours of traveling or being quiet while my daughter slept and healed, I found moments of deep stillness and calm. And out of those moments came insights and solutions. They were not quickie solutions to the problems of the day. They were crystal drops of clarity about who I am and what certain problems and questions mean in relation to that. In the ordinary course of life, I rarely string four quiet *minutes* together before collapsing in weariness. By accepting the space created by what could have seemed just one more demand, I received the gift of reflection.

You needn't wait until a crisis of some kind befalls you to find the space that allows you to get reacquainted with yourself. Once you start looking for them, the potential moments of quiet begin to show up of their own accord. Give your attention to the desire to reflect and the opportunities will come back to you multiplied. They are there waiting to be discovered.

• *Turn off the noise for one half hour a day.* For one week, give yourself a break from the telephone, radio, television, the Internet and the daily newspaper — and don't fill the space elsewhere. Find a place where you can be alone, even if it means taking yourself out for coffee, a walk, a spell in your backyard or a soak in the tub. You may have to advise friends or family that you're not available, lest they make up the noise difference for you. The net result is three and a half hours of quiet in the week, hours in which to hear yourself think.

• *Eat your lunches alone for a week.* If you have obligations — for example, young children or elderly parents in your care — arrange with a relative, friend or hired caregiver to take your place for just an hour or two a day for a single week. If need be, take yourself out of your normal midday scene, whether that's home, the office, the cafeteria or the gym. Not only will you have some quality time with yourself, you will open yourself to the illumination that comes from the simple, but often neglected, act of observing. And what might you observe? Perhaps a bucolic scene and all the whimsy and wonder that nature offers. More likely, people coming and going, talking, chewing, signaling for the check, and moving, moving, moving. People, in other words, just like you.

• *Take a day off.* My friend Beth does this religiously, twice a year. She books a room in her favorite B & B, leaves an emergency-only number with someone she trusts, chooses a book or a sheaf of paper or nothing at all, packs only her overnight clothes, and takes off for 24 hours. Sometimes she wrestles with a thorny dilemma, as when a close friend asked her to write a letter of recommendation for a child Beth knew to be irresponsible and troubled. Sometimes she reads a book she's been fruitlessly salivating over for months. Sometimes she takes long walks and lets her thoughts catch up to her. A hot bath and a stack of her favorite magazines often fill the late afternoon.

She used to pack too much. The items would sit in her stuffed book bag and nag at her for the entire time away, much like the too-busy life she was ignoring for the day. Over time, she has narrowed her bag's contents. She says that the very act of choosing what to pack has become an exercise in self-knowledge and assessment. She doesn't always return enlightened. But she invariably comes back refreshed. And she frequently brings with her one or two good insights that prepare her for the decisions and duties ahead. She has had a chance to think about what matters to her and how that translates into action.

• *Maintain a daily time of meditation or prayer.* This has become a recurrent theme in recent self-help literature. And for good reason. Through the ages, people have found that the habit of time set apart for the spirit becomes a necessary and treasured part of their life. This solitary exercise supplies connectedness, perspective and a daily reminder of a larger reality. Making it a regular habit provides a framework for better knowing yourself, your hopes, fears, abilities and loves.

• *Keep a private record of your thoughts, feelings and reactions.* For many, space for themselves includes pen and paper or the blank page of a journal. In a reflective moment, allow thoughts and feelings about the past and present to flow freely onto the page, without censorship. (You can destroy it when you're done, if need be.) Look for the patterns that appear. Identify points of tension and dissonance that may have grown over time, as well as moments of pleasure. Then consider intentionally the sorts of changes that will promote greater harmony — and wholeness — in the future.

Uncover what matters to you.

How do we achieve self-understanding in relation to all the people and objects that swirl around us? A variety of self-assessment tests have been developed in recent years to help

A survivor's source of perspective

Charles began a daily prayer and meditation time after a serious car accident confined him to a prone position for two months. "At first I couldn't do anything but think," he says. "And for the first time since childhood, I prayed. It was while I was praying that I saw my accident as a picture of my life. It was just push, push, push — too fast, without watching where I was going. I never thought about the meaning of who I am or of what I'll leave behind someday. I mean, I survived the accident. But I'm going to die *sometime*. Maybe living is more than just trying to stay alive."

In the years since that accident, Charles has continued to pray and meditate. He has also made big changes in his medical practice, shifting from a lucrative but demanding private practice to shared responsibilities in a community clinic — work that he finds far more rewarding despite the cut in pay. At the same time, he has joined a canoe club with his children and makes regular trips with them. His prayer and meditation time has become a profound source of strength and perspective. "It's how I set my compass," he says. "It's how I know where to go next."

people discover what will make them happiest. But in many cases, what we need most is to give some undistracted time and focus to what is in our hearts.

• *Write a personal mission statement.* In *Reinventing Your Life,* Jeffrey E. Young and Janet S. Klosko compare this to a blueprint. Living without reference to a personal vision, they say, is like boarding a plane without knowing its destination or running onto a football field without knowing the game plan. Describe in writing what you hope your life will finally add up to. Don't worry about grammar or spelling. Keep writing until you've said everything that comes to your mind. Set it aside for a week. Then come back to it and boil it down to a single paragraph. After another week, reduce the paragraph to a sentence.

• *Develop a "Top Ten List."* Who or what matters most to you in life? List as many items as occur to you. They may be God, people, institutions, beliefs or causes, possessions or plans. After you've come up with a "long" list, eliminate all but the ten most important. Number these items one to ten in order of priority, one being most important, two being next, and so on. How many of the items on your list do you consciously value every day? How does the way you're living reflect the relative importance of each of the items on the list?

• *Conduct a spiritual scavenger hunt.* Sometimes we become so intellectual in our pursuit of self-understanding that we lose touch with what matters to us on a less idea-oriented level. We are, after all, endowed with a spirit as well as a brain, with passions as well as thoughts, with a sense of beauty and goodness, and preferences for certain styles, colors, tastes, places and types of activity. For one week, watch your reactions to your physical environment. Collect objects, photographs, bits of nature, food items, pieces of clothing, postcards, toys or tools that you find especially appealing (not necessarily "beautiful"). Reflect on what you've gathered. Why does each item appeal to you? What sort of emotion does it call up? How would you explain its significance to another person? How much does it reflect what you have included in your life?

• *Interview yourself.* Imagine that you've been invited to meet the person you would most like to get to know. You will have one hour with him or her and you are promised a completely candid conversation. What questions would you ask? Make a list, then mark questions that could apply to you as well. Using a tape recorder, answer each question aloud as though you were speaking to someone who could be trusted absolutely to keep a confidence. Or write out the answers. Save them and reflect on them later.

A teacher's return to center

Ann is a high school math teacher who worked happily for years in a public school. As she became known districtwide, she was earmarked as a prime candidate for administration. The first advancement to department head filled her with pride and pleasure, even though it meant that she spent less time doing what she loved — teaching — and more time coordinating a group of other teachers. Over time, she moved up the administrative ladder, with a growing salary to show for each move, and eventually she hung up her calculator. There followed several years of increasing stress and more frequent letdowns. Ann had less time for her family; she had to work too-long hours doing work she now admits she wasn't well suited for or trained to do and that she frankly did not enjoy.

"It took being fired to bring me to my senses," she says. "I love kids and I love creating fun and crazy ways of teaching that will really speak to kids. I also love my husband and children. I finally remembered that those are my 'bottom line.' Once I got that straight again, all the other decisions became clear."

Intentionality: Doing what I am

Intentionality puts integrity on its feet and gives it a gentle shove forward. Worked together, the two "I" strands of integrity and intentionality create the strong, resilient and luminous thread out of which we can weave a simpler life. But at the heart of intentionality is the recognition that we have and make choices. The more we notice the decisions we make and the better we understand those decisions, the closer we come to creating the life we want.

Recognize the choices you make.

Every day consists of myriad decisions, some self-conscious, many not. For example: I wake up at 7:00 A.M. on a Saturday. What shall I do? Get a good early start or doze for another hour? *I get up.* Read the paper next or take a brisk walk before the day heats up? *Paper.* Breakfast or shower first? *Shower, then breakfast.* What to wear? *Jeans, cotton sweater, loafers.* Pancakes, eggs or cereal? *Cereal.* Spend the morning cleaning the house or do some work I brought home from the office? *Clean.* Afternoon golf tournament on TV or a trip to the local museum with my son? *TV golf, but with my son.* Dinner out or cook on the grill? *Out.* Video in the evening, another chapter of the thriller I'm reading or stop by the neighbors' open house for dessert? *Dessert!* Among these choices lie many smaller ones I don't even realize I'm making.

How many of your daily choices do you notice making? Test it. For just one day, take note of every decision you make. You may want to define "choice" as separate from habits and work disciplines (brushing teeth, clearing the dinner table, leaving for work), but be careful not to eliminate those items that could be changed without harm to health and well-being.

At the end of the day, assess your record. How many choices have you made? Would the number of choices vary between weekdays and weekends, home and vacation? How many choices reflect the beliefs and values undergirding your life or a divergence from those values? How many would you usually make without thinking? Would you change any now, looking back on the day?

TO LIVE INTENTIONALLY

Recognize the choices you make.

Notice your internal language.

Turn off autopilot.

Every action or nonaction is, in fact, a choice. Only when we recognize and take responsibility for the choices we are making can we move on to a conscious, intentional life.

Notice your internal language.

In *The Seven Habits of Highly Effective People,* Stephen Covey stresses the profound effect language has on how we think of ourselves. He distinguishes especially between reactive and proactive language. "There's nothing I can do" is reactive. "Let's look at our alternatives" is proactive. "I have to do that" is reactive. "I will choose an appropriate response" is proactive. "I must" vs. "I prefer." "If only" vs. "I will."

We often assume the language and attitudes of inevitability. "This is the way it is." "I'm stuck." "I'm trapped." "I can't." We forget that much of what our life has become has grown out of our daily choices. And what we do with where we are now is also a matter of choice. Jeff, for example, is in a bad relationship with more grief than joy, but he is not stuck in it. He chooses to continue the association, but he could choose differently. Perhaps he has weighed every imaginable option, and he has good reasons for putting up with the relational frustrations and pain. In that case, he is living intentionally, and he can take satisfaction in the active choice he has made. He has put himself in position to actively consider ways to improve the quality of the time he spends both with that individual and without.

Turn off autopilot.

There are routines I practice with such regularity that I find myself doing them without thinking. I suddenly wonder halfway through my day whether I brushed my teeth after breakfast, and I only know for sure by checking whether my toothbrush is damp. It's a common experience, what we call "autopilot." To live intentionally, we have to turn off autopilot, and that can be hard to do. But it isn't impossible. It simply takes practice.

- *Stand on your head.* Western culture seems disposed to view reality in terms of either-or. Yet rarely do only two possibilities exist in response to a question or choice. For one hour, each time a decision needs to be made, dismiss the first set of two options that occurs to you. Look at the decision from at least one completely new angle. Come up with three or more other possible choices. It doesn't matter if they are fantastic or impossible in the real world. Just don't jump to the automatic solution or stop thinking about new alternatives. Instead, turn it around — or more to the point, turn yourself around. It's challenging to defy gravity, but you'll get a fresh infusion of blood to your decision making.

- *Live counterintuitively.* Often our choices are actually *reactions.* We are hit with a force, so to speak, and we answer with equal or greater force. Intentional living requires that we learn to replace *reaction* with *action,* and that means pausing and considering options that do not come naturally to us.

Myra tells the story of her brother, Peter. At every family gathering, Peter made himself the center of attention. If someone else had a story to tell, Peter would quickly find a way to introduce a story of his own that would turn all eyes back to him. "My reaction after a lifetime with him," Myra recalls, "was to ignore him every chance I got. I didn't want to feed that monster ego of his."

Myra intuitively resisted giving her brother the attention he wanted, because the way he demanded it was inappropriate. She came to avoid any family gathering that included her brother. It saved her aggravation, but she soon felt guilty and left out. Then someone suggested that she try giving Peter attention *before* he sought it. For Myra, this idea was counterintuitive. It didn't come naturally, but she decided to give it a try. "I began to look for things in Peter that I admired and made a point of telling him," she says. "Other family members followed suit. Oddly, it didn't make him more self-centered. He thanked us for our encouragement. He even looked for ways to make us feel good about ourselves."

The first choice that occurs to us may not be one that allows us to be in harmony with our spirit. In an automatic effort to avoid reinforcing her brother's poor behavior, Myra isolated herself and resented him all the more. When she responded intentionally to meet the needs her brother was unconsciously displaying, she simplified both her inner life and time spent with extended family.

• *Tap your passions.* At the heart of each of us resides a fiery enthusiasm waiting to erupt. As we mature, we're taught to firmly harness this energy. But it is in this molten core that we find our principles and values and discover the most authentic expressions of who we are. Ride the tide of enthusiasm when it overflows. Let it lead you to a deeper understanding of yourself and a greater joy in being alive. If you feel the urge to express it on a canvas, sign up for a painting class. If you feel like dancing, roll up the rug, turn up the stereo, and let your feet and body, arms and head move as they will. Sing in the shower. Run in the park. Make love in the middle of the day. Plant a tree or bake an apple pie. Give yourself permission to adore life, and give yourself up to the passion of joyful activity.

• *Explore new directions.* The expression "Lower than a snake's belly in a wagon wheel rut" has always tickled my fancy because it describes the depression of an unimaginative life so well. We "get into a rut" and all of life takes on the color and texture of old mud. But staying in the rut is a choice, like everything else in life. One of my daughters once offered me her own list of 27 "lessons for living." My two favorites apply here: Always sing the way you sing when you're singing your best; and have (at least) one adventure a week. Get out of the rut, slither on up into the wagon and get ready for the ride of your life.

• *Practice the art of composting.* Inevitably as we live more intentionally, we discover habits and attitudes that don't belong in a life simply lived. We cling to them because they're familiar and therefore comfortable or because we are lazy and don't want to exert the energy required to change them. Or, conversely, we grab them by the neck and enact murder, full of indignation and self-criticism. Personally, I prefer to consider old, outdated thoughts and actions along an organic model. They've had their day, for better or worse, and now they're like a garden's stubble. We can plow them under and allow them to decompose without rancor. In that way they come to enrich the living material of our present and future.

Nine months are required for a woman to bring a baby from the glint in her partner's eye to a squalling, suckling new person who's ready to be out and about. It can easily take another nine months to return to her pre-pregnancy state. In fact, she'll never really return. She'll move on to a new place, even though her size and shape may return to some approximation of its former self. In the meantime, however, she has added new depths and joys, understanding, and connectedness.

So too when we simplify our lives. We didn't begin in this state of complexity. We took a good long time to get here. Once we start the adventure of creating a simpler life, we begin the journey not back but forward to a deeper, richer life that reflects what is best and most important in and to us. We won't get there overnight. We only need to keep moving in that direction, to begin again each new day and anticipate with enthusiasm what's next.

Balanced Time

"Time was a river," writes Margaret A. Robinson in A Woman of Her Tribe,

"not a log to be sawed into lengths." We have a finite amount of measurable time

in which to live out our present existence. But can time be more, as Robinson

suggests, than the seconds, minutes, hours or days in which we count it off? A

simpler life offers the potential to shape our experience of time, to live in harmony

with it and make it our ally.

It's a funny thing about time. I've talked to a lot of people in the last couple of years about the idea of a simpler life. It doesn't seem to matter how much activity, business, creativity or relating a person packs into 24 hours. For some, it feels like a squeeze, and they are always running to catch up, stretching to meet commitments, frazzled, frenzied, frayed at the seams. For others, it's a great adventure, a full life, going for all the gusto they can get. What makes the difference?

In the movie *IQ,* a character named Ed meets Albert Einstein's niece, Kathryn, with whom Ed will eventually form a romantic relationship. But he knows from first sight that she is the one for him. "How do you know?" asks Uncle Albert. Ed replies that when they met, everything slowed down. As though he were working on honing a machine part (Ed is a mechanic) and all of time and life focused on that single act in that single span of time; and he could feel that it would fit perfectly. The moment with Kathryn lasted as long as it needed to, and left Ed filled with certainty and satisfaction. To Einstein, the great guru of relativity, this was a convincing argument. That Ed could, in a moment, live not only the moment but also an infinity of future moments that defined a burgeoning relationship and watched its blossoming was not only plausible but convincing.

Most of us have experienced isolated moments or periods of time such as Ed describes. It is almost as though the very nature of time and its passing has temporarily changed. We kick back on a vacation that seems endless, the hours stretching unaccountably, the clock barely moving. Or we work with utter concentration on a project, soaring through the process with no perception of minutes sliding away beneath us, and emerge with a shock to discover that we have accomplished an extraordinary amount in a relatively short time span or have passed hours in what felt like a heartbeat.

It is, in its essence, time of the highest quality, what we might call timeless time. Uncomplicated by distractions and disruptions, timeless time occurs when we are most in tune with ourselves, our abilities, our infatuations. The great athletes experience it in the midst of a game brilliantly played. Writers and artists find it at the height of the creative process, when the muse strikes and their art and their spirit come together. Teachers live it in those moments of true communication with their students, when lights turn on and epiphanies follow. Lovers discover it in the rare, blessed spaces of true, undiverted intimacy.

Let's get right to the heart of it. The experience of timeless time is uncommon for most of us. Instead, time becomes "the enemy" that we're constantly working to defeat. We want to stop the clock so that we can accomplish everything on the list, enjoy the good times while they last, avoid the inevitable effects of aging.

Timeless time eludes us. We need to ask the fundamental question of ourselves — where does our time go?

I recently had a conversation with Jack, a business associate of mine, that deeply saddened me. He was late delivering an important contract to me, which put in jeopardy the project for which the contract had to be drawn. He called to explain. To his credit, he took responsibility for his lateness. I must have sounded sympathetic (I was), because he then went on to say how difficult it is to do his job in the corporate environment.

"There's no TIME!" he exploded. He described his work as a veritable three-ring circus of unnecessary meetings, endless paperwork and habitual job anxiety.

"But I have to remind myself that this is only a small part of the journey," he said, before offering this final explanation. "The way I see it," he continued, "life is a bad bus stop. It's a nasty part of the journey, but it isn't our destination."

I agree with Jack in part. I believe as he does that there's more to existence than this moment or even this mortal life. I don't believe, however, that for most of us this life needs to be a "bad bus stop" on the journey. Perhaps Jack has insufficient time for all that he needs to do. Most of us feel that periodically. Some of us feel it chronically. The question is, does it have to be that way? I believe not. Change is possible, whether it's a change in our circumstance or a change in our attitude.

You may think you know where the time goes when you find yourself coming up short. But are you sure? "I can't fit one more thing into my daily life," I hear myself saying at the end of a long day. "I'm drowning! God forbid anything unusual should come up — a sick child, a broken water heater, an unexpected guest, a last-minute work assignment. Never mind something I'd really *like* to do!" That is the language of my *feelings* about time. It may not be the *reality*.

In Jack's case, his feeling that his life is a "bad bus stop" may reflect the truth about his present reality or it may not. Sadly, though, that feeling has become the ruling voice in Jack's head, and as a result he lives as though he were helpless, a victim. He could choose to live differently. If he cannot change the environment in which he works, he may be able to change his job (don't panic, people do it every day), or he may change his attitude about it. Either way, he is stepping out of the reactive mode to live *intentionally*. Any change that is based on who he is will create greater *integrity*, and his experience of time will be more satisfying — more timeless.

This is true of all of us. We may have to do battle with perennial time wasters in our lives. We may have to take the first important steps toward conquering a lifelong habit of procrastination. Or we may have to reckon with the inappropriate demands made on our time by others or the negative effects of our own inefficiency.

Life offers no more precious gift than the days and hours and minutes of our existence. Just ask someone about time who has been diagnosed with a terminal illness; or who is celebrating a seventieth, eightieth or ninetieth birthday; or who has recently lost someone they deeply loved.

We don't have to be within hailing distance of mortal danger to appreciate the preciousness of life. As we give a small, regular part of our time to reflection, we clean the lens of our long-range vision. We become more adept at *assessing* the way we arrange our commitments and activities, rest and recreation. We learn to *identify* the time gobblers that don't "fit" who we are and what we value and to eliminate or adjust them. And we have the clarity to *reinvent* the use of our time with integrity.

Assessing your time

One of the first exercises that people trying to lose weight are asked to do is to keep a food journal. Doug talks about his early conversations with his doctor on the subject. "I eat almost nothing!" he claimed. And he believed it. But when he followed the doctor's prescription to record every morsel of food that passed his lips, he was astonished. "I had trouble even keeping the journal at first. I'd eat without noticing," Doug confesses. "My boss keeps a dish of Peanut M&M's on the mail table that I pass fifty times a day. I have a bag of jumbo pretzels in my desk that I dig into when the tension rises. My colleagues and I like to head over to a lunch buffet — all you can eat. Get it?"

Just so with time for many of us. We think we know why the days are so full, and we think that it's an inevitable function of modern life that we end up with so little time for the activities and relationships that mean the most to us. Not so. Remember: We've made a series of choices to arrive where we are. Making a different set of choices can change the way we spend our time to better reflect who we are and what matters to us.

TO TRACK YOUR TIME

Keep a journal.

Make a weekly schedule.

Create a time sheet.

First, however, we need real information — the facts about where our time actually goes. The only effective way to gather that information is to track our time, just as Doug tracked his food consumption. Consider one of the following methods for logging the way you use time. Choose the one that seems easiest to you. Don't worry about creating anything fancy. The last thing you need is to add this exercise as a burden to your already full life. Keep it simple and commit to doing it for just a week. After a week, you may want more information. If so, keep it up a while longer.

Keep a journal.

Try carrying a small spiral notebook around with you all day every day for a week. Or even better, find a blank daily planner that already has the days divided into hours and half hours and carry it in your pocket or purse. Begin recording how you spend your time when you wake up ("6:00 A.M. — rise and shine"), and simply jot down the time whenever you change activity ("6:30 — jog; 7:45 — shower & shave; 8:30 — breakfast; 9:15 — phone calls: Dad, exterminators, doctor for checkup"). The more specific you are, the more helpful the information may be later, but even a general record will be revealing. Don't forget to record the time you use to pick up mail, open and read it. Include the time it takes to choose what you will wear and to dress, to change into casuals later, and to put clothes away at the end of the day. If you shave, blow-dry your hair, put on makeup or trim your mustache, write it down! Include every trip to the store, gas station, local café, friend's house or coffee machine.

Make a weekly schedule.

If keeping a constant record seems cumbersome, try creating a grid for an entire week, then filling it out according to how you spend your time. You may be able to do this in one sitting, but you'll probably find it more accurate to fill in each day, right before you go to bed. In any case, you should include everything.

An insomniac seeks a time cure

Paula knew she needed to take a serious look at her life and health when she fell into a trough of insomnia. She never had trouble falling asleep — as the manager of her own small business, she did enough in any given day to tire her out. But after an hour or two, she would awaken with her mind racing and her heart pounding, "as though my body was on 'red alert,'" she says.

Paula tried a whole series of sleep tricks. They'd work for a while and then they'd fail her. It wasn't until a close friend suggested that Paula keep a time journal, to see whether stress or overwork "might" be related to her sleeplessness, that she confessed to herself that she had let the days of her life get out of control. "But I had to see it in black and white," she recalls. "I had to look at page after page of days loaded with work and responsibilities to recognize that I didn't even have time to sit down and browse through a magazine without feelings of panic overtaking me."

With the journal before her, Paula has begun to reshape her time. She has said no to a number of flexible commitments. And she has called off "red alert."

Nothing is too small to note. This type of record provides an at-a-glance look not only at the daily particulars but at patterns in your use of time as well.

Create a time sheet.

This alternative starts with categories instead of the clock. Make a master list of all the component parts of your daily life — sleep, meal preparation, eating, cleaning up, family interaction, work, reading, fitness, driving, shopping, home and car maintenance, recreation, and so forth. Then estimate the amount of time weekly spent on each. Be as accurate as possible. The point is to have a realistic view of your present use of time.

Eventually, you'll want to use some of your daily reflection time to study whichever record you've made. Pick a time when you aren't under the gun or tired. Focus on what you've recorded until you can almost picture your time in three dimensions, with bulges, pinches, ragged spots and flat areas. Give your emotions room to surface. "Feel" the good times; "suffer" the stressful, unproductive or uncomfortable times. Your visceral reactions will help you to better understand what belongs in your life and what doesn't. But don't rush to conclusions. You may feel upset when you consider something in your schedule that is deeply meaningful to you and belongs there but is not getting its fair share of your time.

You need to exercise feelings, brain and soul as you consider your time record. Evaluate what you *feel* in terms of what you *know* about your choices and intentions. Then listen to your own internal voice. Are there moments of timeless time in your present experience? If not presently, how about in the past? What were you doing? With whom? In what circumstances (place, season, phase of life)? Make a list of those times.

When I did this, I was amazed at what I discovered. While I had been setting my sights on the "big" goals of life, the great joys and lasting connections were surfacing and developing in the tiny, unexceptional moments of my experience. I caught them out of the corner of my eye, but once caught, they lit the brightest fires.

Identifying time troubles

Even after you've studied the record you've created to track your time, you may not immediately identify the misfits in your life, but that does *not* mean they don't exist. One helpful way to identify them is to ask four simple questions for each item in your daily life:

1. *Does this contribute to my life goals and values?*
2. *Does it enhance my health or happiness?*
3. *Does it have to be done now?*
4. *Does it ever have to be done?*

If an item rates four yeses, you're dealing with something that probably deserves to be a priority in your life. It is important and urgent. You will identify other aspects of your experience, however, that get three, two or one yes. While these, too, may continue to warrant some of your time, they may not deserve as much time as you're giving them now. Pay special attention to any item for which you answer *no, no, no, no*. This is a time trouble, and it deserves one more question and a ruthlessly honest answer: *Why do I give any of my time to this?*

Time troubles take different forms, but they have one thing in common. They use up time that could be put to much better use. Identifying the troubles goes a long way toward robbing them of their power over your time.

Eliminate time wasters.

Time wasters are the things that never have to be done, at least by you. They may be chores, habits or escape activities. They may even be false courtesy — as in staying on the phone with a telemarketer when you know you don't want anything they have to sell, or attending a function you have no purpose at or interest in because someone invited you personally.

Time wasters are intensely personal critters. They have no one shape or size; sometimes what wastes one person's time adds vibrancy, relaxation, joy or quality to another's. On the other hand,

A working woman counts the cost of a time waster

When Andrea tried the exercise of tracking her time, she was shocked at the number of hours in a single week she was giving to electronic games. "I come home after work and turn on the computer to get my E-mail. I'm tired and I don't feel like doing much, so I open up the Klondike file [a computer solitaire game] just for a while. The thing is, 'a while' has turned into three, four, even five hours a week."

Meanwhile, Andrea complained about a chronic backache that added to her feeling of fatigue and took away from her general enjoyment of life. The doctor told her an old back injury was going to keep her in pain unless she did some regular stomach and back exercises and stretches. "I kept telling the doc that I didn't have time to do them," Andrea admits. "And as long as I kept wasting time on that computer game, it was more or less true. Now I realize that sitting at the computer those extra hours was not only using the time I needed for the exercises, it was actually adding to my back pain."

some time wasters seem universally dispensable. I have wasted time changing clothes two or three times a day when one right choice could have done for the whole day. My friend wastes time dicing the bread he throws out the door for the birds to eat. Do the birds care? A former boss used to waste time micromanaging his work team by redoing all their work.

TO DEBUG YOUR TIME

Eliminate time wasters.

Deflate time bloaters.

Recognize time eroders.

Opening junk mail, moving piles of clutter from one surface to another, watching hours of television a day, playing the delaying game with any one of a hundred tiny reorganizations — all of these creep into our lives and stand in the way of timeless time.

Begin by finding the time wasters in your schedule. Focus on just one. Try *not doing it* for a day. (Instead of hanging on through that phone solicitation, say, "I never accept these calls," and hang up. Or hang up in the first place.) Continue *not doing it* for a week, a month. Then take on another time waster. And another. Keep it up until you use them up.

Deflate time bloaters.

These things should take less time than they do. They can be done more efficiently, done less often, delegated or consolidated.

Some people, for example, make many small shopping trips — to the grocery store, the hardware store, the clothing store, a convenience store — when they could accomplish as much in a single, regularly scheduled trip. With better planning, they could save time, money, wear and tear, and fuel. The same may apply to trips upstairs and downstairs in your home. It may apply to paying bills, returning phone calls, grading papers, visiting clients, preparing meals, writing reports or doing the laundry.

Look for time bloaters in your day. Choose just one and think of at least three ways to cut down on the time it takes. Pick the way that appeals most to you and try it for a week. If it works, keep it up. If not, try another way. Once the new way has become *your* way, choose another time bloater and repeat the process.

Recognize time eroders.

You probably won't find any of these actually written down in your record, no matter how you have chosen to track your time. These are our habits of thought and attitude that eat our time without us knowing it. They've become unconscious companions that distract us and weigh us down. Like rain or wind on an unplanted hillside, they wear at us and carry off priceless hours, while adding nothing to the quality of our journey.

• *Many of us lose enormous amounts of time to worry.* When I was a teenager, wallowing in some adolescent angst, my mother would invariably respond, "Don't trouble trouble. Most of it never happens anyway." It took me years to understand the wisdom of that little aphorism. Our worries are based on what might happen, not on reality. If we have legitimate concerns about the future, we need to discover whether there is any action we should be taking now and take it. The rest is wasted time.

• *Worry's complement in the past tense is regret.* It's hard to calculate the emotional currency squandered on this emotion. Not that we should blithely move on from bad choices, immoral acts or damaging behavior without feeling remorse. The basic difference between the good citizen and the hardened criminal may be the ability to regret productively — to use the emotion to change behavior. Feel remorse, if it's appropriate. Make amends, if possible, and find ways to do better in the future. Then shed the regret and get on with living morally and conscientiously.

• *Negativity, in one form or another, eats the heart out of our time if we let it.* It may take the shape of jealousy, when we waste energy calculating our worth in comparison to someone else's, in dollars, looks, talent or relationships. It may be a grudge or resentment that we nurse with grim determination, using our creativity to plan revenge or angry rhetoric. It may be self-doubt, fear of failure or rejection, disappointment, or guilt. No matter what form negativity takes, it leads us to put off those things we long to accomplish or enjoy because, in some way, we believe that we don't deserve, or couldn't possibly earn, the best that life has to offer.

All of these time eroders need to be exposed to the light of day. In your reflection time, allow worries, regrets and negativity to surface. Write individual instances of them down. Choose one at a time. Write it on a separate, clean piece of paper. Face it squarely. Consider whether it calls for any action (a fallback plan, an apology, a session with a counselor, a trip to a 12-step program), and if so, make a plan. Leave space on the page both to record the plan of action and to report the outcome. When you have done both, fold up the page and put it in an envelope labeled "Eroders." Leave it there. Every time the thought or attitude returns, visualize it on the paper and mentally put it back into the envelope.

Reinventing your time

Some years ago, a psychologist, a documentary filmmaker and a university business school professor put their heads together on the subject of creativity. As part of their collaboration, Daniel Goleman, Paul Kaufman and Michael Ray investigated the mentality of some of this century's most innovative inventors. They concluded this: "The ability to see things in a fresh way is vital to the creative process, and that ability rests on the willingness to question any and all assumptions."

You've made yourself conscious of the way you use your time, and you've begun to take daily steps to eliminate or change aspects of it that work against you. Now you are ideally placed to think in more creative terms about how to invent a life that makes the most of the time you've been given to live. Take a quiet moment to consider the internal timekeeper that regulates your body rhythms. All time is not equal in an individual's experience. We all have natural, daily highs and lows. Try the "Mapping Your Time Temperament" exercise on the facing page. Then go back to the record you've made of your time. Question all the assumptions that have led to your current use of time. Give yourself permission to invent your own best-case scenario and to look for ways to transform your present experience to move closer and closer to it.

Put first things in prime time.

Give your best time first to who or what is most important to you. I'm a morning person. Yet for years, I spent my most energetic, early hours getting the day's lesser work out of the way. I'd straighten up, make lists, run errands, make phone calls, read the newspaper. By the time I sat down to write, create a lesson plan or develop a speech, I was tired and felt like taking a break.

With some juggling, I began moving lesser activities to times of lower energy, thereby freeing up my best time for the work that mattered most to me and produced the most meaningful results.

Mapping Your Time Temperament

Start with a blank schedule or daily planner. You can use different color highlighters or a simple code to fill in the times with the following general information about how you tick.

- *Prime time.*

    Highlight your own best times in a given day. When are you most alert? Least in demand? Most creative? Least distracted?

- *Survival time.*

    Block off reasonable, regular time for sleeping, eating, bathing, brushing, exercise, reflection and any other components of personal health that you currently practice.

- *Committed time.*

    Mark in time that is presently not yours to decide or that is already allotted (work hours, church hours, shared mealtime, commute time, gym time, class time).

- *Discretionary time.*

    You don't have to do anything to allocate this. This is all the time that is left over.

Don't worry that some of the categories overlap. The idea is to create a reasonable map of how you can go on from self-knowledge to intentional change. At present, you may be using prime time for activities that you could do in your off-peak periods. With some imagination and a will to take charge, you can make the most of the time you have — not necessarily to get more done or to fit more in, but rather to live the way you truly desire.

Making such changes isn't easy. There are reasons why you have perennially put off what matters most to you. As with every other step toward living more simply, try a small change at a time. Your motivation to keep going will grow with each success.

You may also have to educate friends, family and associates to the fact that you are not available at prime time. Or you may have to inform the "whats" in your life — unfinished business, chores, letters or bills, belongings — that the people in your life come first. Even finding reflection time may present a challenge.

Practice doing just one thing.

The February 2, 1996, entry on "The Little Zen Calendar" was a quote from Alan Watts that reads: "Zen does not confuse spirituality with thinking about God while one is peeling potatoes. Zen spirituality is just to peel the potatoes." Sylvia Boorstein expands this idea in her book *Don't Just Do Something, Sit There*. "Mindfulness, seeing clearly," she says, "means awakening to the happiness of the uncomplicated moment. We complicate moments. Hardly anything happens without the mind spinning it up into an elaborate production. It's the elaboration that makes life more difficult than it needs to be."

We don't have to be Zen masters to appropriate the wisdom in these messages. If you've managed to move your most important activities into prime time, your next discipline is to practice doing only that activity at that time. People who care for small children get into the habit, out of necessity, of seeing out of eyes in the back of their heads, listening and responding to two or three conversations at the same time, anticipating trouble and preventing injury. In fact, they are *doing one thing* — it just happens to have many facets simultaneously in play. But many of us become nanny to a hundred ongoing concerns that we tend at all times as though they were children in our care. We let them distract us, no matter what we're doing, and we lose the focus and joy and simplicity of being where we are and doing what we're doing.

TO TRANSFORM YOUR TIME

Put first things in prime time.

Practice doing just one thing.

Practice flexible time.

Plan to play.

Promote "potential" time.

No matter what we are doing, or when, if we give it our full attention, the quality of the time we give it increases measurably. Are you pulling weeds? Then notice the shape and smell of the vegetation. Glory in the ground you are clearing and the beauty your work creates. Concentrate on the nutrients you are freeing for the plants that remain. Watch with pleasure the growing heap of plant material in your bucket. Are you opening the mail? Imagine who prepared the mailing, what they hoped to accomplish, how they may have pictured you receiving it. Take pride in dispatching the day's pile into trash, file and "to be answered" basket. Congratulate yourself on staying with the job until it's done. Consider how to eliminate the mail you don't want.

Practice flexible time.

There are aspects to everyone's time that simply cannot be planned. Emergencies happen, unusual circumstances arise, unexpected opportunities present themselves. It's important to choose how you want to use your time. It's equally important to prepare yourself for the unexpected and to practice bending and flexing to meet it.

Don't be surprised when your time doesn't go as you've planned. Accept in advance that this may happen, and be prepared to make adjustments. By keeping a realistic perspective, you will help to offset the feelings of frustration and defeat that can otherwise escalate a necessary change of plans into what Robert Pirsig, in *Zen and the Art of Motorcycle Maintenance,* called a "gumption trap." That's the mindset that says, "It isn't perfect, so now I can't get on with it."

On the other hand, don't make bending and flexing your automatic response to the distractions and time eaters that arise. The trick is to recognize which changes are unavoidable and/or desirable and which are impositions of other people's needs or preferences. The former call for flexibility, the latter for firmness.

Plan to play.

John is a builder. He works long hours, and his workday doesn't end when he leaves a building site. He has future bids to prepare, payrolls to meet, materials to order, invoices to pay, taxes to track and problems on present projects to solve. He spends all his time as though he were running to catch up, and he feels as if life is somehow passing him by. When I ask him why he doesn't get out and do something for fun, he says, "I can't. I feel too guilty, because I know I haven't finished everything that has to be done."

Many people, like John, have difficulty justifying playtime. And yet it's that free and easy time that gives us space to reconnect and recharge. Look at the word *recreation*. We use  the word to describe any activity that isn't work or sleep. We tend to think that it is what we do *if* we have any time left over after all the must-do's have been taken care of. I, like a great many others, am a firm believer in the power of language to shape our perceptions. And I'm convinced that we've lost the real sense of the word *recreation*. The word's Latin root means "restoration to health" and refers to "refreshment of strength and spirits after work." If we look up the verb form, *recreate,* in the dictionary, we read "to give new life or freshness to," which puts a special spin on the idea of recreation as "amusement or diversion."

Does this sound like a frill or an extra to you? If so, you've been indoctrinated by a money-hungry, work-obsessed society that is going to wring you out like a wet mop and hang you up to die young. It's time to rethink recreation.

Neil Fiore contends, in *The Now Habit,* that the key to happier, more productive work time is proactively scheduling playtime. "Attempting to skimp on holidays, rest and exercise," says Fiore, "leads to suppression of the spirit and motivation as life begins to look like all spinach and no dessert." A guilt-free approach to having fun — gardens, sports, crafts, reading, painting, making love, hiking, meeting friends, traveling — helps us to stop postponing life in all its fullness. The simpler life is a balanced life. We may need to make adjustments, but it's a life we can have.

Promote "potential" time.

This is the time saved for ongoing reflection, change and growth — the time for discovering and feeding the potential in life and yourself. It's the spiritual equivalent of recharging a battery or filling a tank with gas. We may feel that we don't have time for it, but without it, we'll find eventually that we're stopped in our tracks.

If you don't presently allow for potential time, try finding just 30 minutes in the week. Maybe you'll want to set this time aside at the start of the week, to gain perspective before charging ahead. Maybe you'll want to place it at the end of the week, so you can reflect on where you've been and what has happened. I know many people who have scheduled potential time into their lives.

Not one of them has ever regretted it, and almost all of them have increased it over time, as they've come to value the insights, joys and balance it adds to their daily experience.

Timeless time is both a requisite and a reward of living a simpler life. In Sue Bender's marvelous book *Plain and Simple,* she describes one of many days spent with the women of the Amish community. "The women moved through the day unhurried," she says. "There was no rushing to finish so they could get on to the 'important things.' For them, it was all important." Bender describes herself as "obsessed with the Amish. Objectively, it made no sense. I, who worked hard at being special, fell in love with a people who valued being ordinary." She describes her prior experience of time as "a burden." But among the Amish, she says, "time was full and generous. It was as if they had uncovered a way to be in time, to be a part of time, to have a harmonious relation with time."

It could be that timeless time, like happiness, will come upon us when we least expect it. But that doesn't mean that we can't encourage both. Create an environment in which what you value shapes what you do, and timelessness, harmony and happiness will follow.

Simply Together

Togetherness. It can make our hearts swell and it can make them break. It often defines what we do, where we go, how we live. At its best, it is the grand web of human connections that lifts each of us out of our aloneness and makes us somehow larger than ourselves. But our need for connection is the source of many of life's complexities as well. The challenge is to simplify our togetherness.

Like it or not, we enter this life equipped with an umbilical cord. We begin in a relationship with our mother, and from moment one on the "outside," we add one relationship after another. Of necessity, we have biological parents (and sometimes surrogates), siblings and extended family. We belong to the community in which we live. We are citizens of a nation, members of voluntary organizations, employees or employers, students or teachers, parents, aunts, uncles, grandparents, and children. Our days and nights are made up of hundreds of psychological and relational transactions.

And here's an immutable fact of relationship math. While one person plus one other person may equal two people, the addition of one more does NOT equal three. Every additional relationship complicates the dynamics of relating by multiples. Ask anyone who decides to have a child. Or a *second* child. Or a second *spouse*. In fact, our relationships with others cause some of the knottiest complexities of our daily lives.

If that sounds like the scary news, here's the underlying salve. We need one another. The human race would long since have ceased without togetherness, and most of what makes life wonderful and meaningful grows out of our connectedness to one another. No sane person, if given the choice, would opt for a life in which all other human beings had been eliminated. Relationships are worth the complexities. Even more, they're worth the effort to simplify, because they become all the more helpful and meaningful and delicious in the process.

Begin once again with self-assessment. Recognize where you are right now — both in general (how you tend to relate to others) and specifically (what the current state of your relationships is). This understanding is your foundation, and you'll want it to be sound and strong.

Starting where you are

Consider two important elements in how you relate. You might think of them as your *temperament* — your "style" of relating — and your *temperature* — your "state" of well-being. In the case of temperament, you are dealing with the basic ingredients of your own personality, whether you are an introvert or an extrovert, whether you are more inclined to action or reflection, whether you deal best with many casual acquaintances or a few deep friendships, and so on. In the case of temperature, you're looking at the quality and emotional health of your active relationships, and the extent to which you are true to yourself within them. Reflecting on both of these facets will make it far easier to know what kinds of changes will serve you best.

Make a personal people profile.

I live with an introvert. He loves to be alone. True contentment for him is to be quiet for hours or days or — so it seems — weeks. I'm a people person. A good conversation is like light and air and food to me. I get a positive charge out of "together" time. After more than two decades together, we had come to an uneasy, not entirely cordial, standoff over these differences. We each had resigned ourselves to the fact that the other had some serious character flaws.

Then, for separate professional reasons, we both dipped into the book *You Just Don't Understand,* by Deborah Tannen, in which Tannen looks at conflicts that grow out of differences in communication styles and emotional needs. Our individual readings produced a mutual revelation. What we had seen to be "right" in ourselves turned out to have a lot to do with our respective genders, personalities and upbringings. What we had seen to be "wrong" in one another was, more often than not, simply different and in fact quite common. With more understanding came new perspectives on our differences, and the common ground we needed to respect and enjoy one another more expanded. We are still learning how to balance our shared life to accommodate, even to capitalize on, those differences. But we're also learning the benefits of cooperation and a sense of humor.

TO BEGIN

Make a personal people profile.

Perform a relational checkup.

When we begin to recognize our own unique qualities and characteristics, it often becomes easier to recognize and appreciate the same in others. It also makes it easier to devise ways to live together that enhance everyone's lives.

Ask yourself a few fundamental questions. For example:

- *What is your relational style? Do you draw energy from others (extrovert) or feel drained by others (introvert)?*
- *How many hours in a given day do you need and/or desire the company of others?*
- *What do you value most in other people? What do you most respect?*
- *What relationships in the past have contributed most to your health? Happiness? Personal growth? Ability to contribute to our world?*
- *What relationships in the past have detracted from your joy? Satisfaction? Self-esteem? Productivity?*

Write the answers down. Or speak your thoughts out loud into a tape recorder. Or use what Sarah Ban Breathnach, in *Simple Abundance*, calls the "illustrated discovery journal": find photographic images, printed words, lyrics, poems, greeting cards and artwork that describe for you the answers to the questions. In one way or another, make a visceral — instinctive rather than intellectual — record.

Remember that the answers to these questions can change as you change. Although your fundamental personality may be "hardwired" at birth, various facets of human existence — experience, nurture, education, religious and philosophical beliefs, and your own will — exert powerful influences on you. From one season of life to another, you deal with a changing set of needs, circumstances and people. Relationships — who, what kind, when, how much — are as much a process as personal growth, and even life itself. What worked a few years ago may not be appropriate now. Over the course of a lifetime, many relational habits and patterns can profitably be made, broken and remade. We refine our understanding of what matters as we mature, and we discover the longer-range effects of particular actions and attitudes in relation to others over time.

Perform a relational checkup.

After you take stock of your relational personality and past, you can begin to give yourself a relational checkup. Imagine the doctor performing an overall physical exam. She looks for signs of unhealthiness, examines tender spots, checks out swellings, notices losses of luster or vitality. You can do the same with your relationships.

Begin by making a list of the people who figure most often or importantly in your present life. Then ask yourself a new set of questions, keeping these people in mind. Be as honest as you can. This is tricky territory, and sometimes we so successfully compensate for pain, anger and frustration that we fool ourselves. We perform the little cover-ups that keep us numb.

- *Are there areas of ongoing tension in some current relationship?*
- *Do you regularly feel put upon, put down or put out in a given relationship? In general?*
- *Does a particular group get-together fill you with dread?*
- *Do you routinely come away from a certain association depressed, drained or discouraged about yourself, your life or your world?*
- *Does the very idea of one more social commitment make you want to throw a bag over your head and hide?*

A "Yes" response to any of the questions above will help you to pinpoint the areas where you may want to start looking for a simpler way. For every "Yes," elaborate on the "who," "what," "where," "when" and "how." Be a good reporter and get as many facts and specifics down as you can. Accept no vague answers from yourself. If you sense that you have trouble seeing your own hiding techniques, ask a trusted friend to listen to your responses (minus any reference to him or her, obviously) and to point out the ones that don't really give complete answers or that don't ring "true."

Preparing for change

Only a fool sets out on a journey with no thought about what he
or she might face along the way. As you move forward, equipped
with some self-knowledge and conscious of areas of your
relational life that you would like to reshape, you should also
remember that you don't go into the business of change alone.
Any human relationship requires at least two persons.
Any change in a relationship affects at least
two persons and will call up a response in
both. Keeping a few predictable responses
to change in mind may help you to move
ahead with confidence and peace
of mind.

Expect resistance.

Resistance from others is a sure thing. When
we change, in effect we force the people to
whom we are connected to change as well,
because they have to change in relation to us.
Change is almost always threatening,
especially when it's happening in someone
else. It doesn't seem to matter that the changes we are initiating
make us happier or calmer or more fulfilled (at least at first). We
have automatically become less predictable, perhaps less

understandable and certainly less familiar. "I thought I knew you!" is, in our culture, a veiled insult, implying that change is a betrayal. But if we are people of integrity, this resistance should not matter, any more than a painful therapy matters on the road to recovery. Only keep in mind that the people who know us well may suddenly question whether they really do know us. At best, that's uncomfortable.

It's also okay. We can ease the way for those around us if we keep in mind how it looks from their point of view and find ways to inform, reassure and include them.

> **WHEN YOU START TO CHANGE**
>
> *Expect resistance.*
>
> *Have a heart.*
>
> *Share the adventure.*
>
> *Expect some intermediate complications.*

Have a heart.

Recognize how scary the journey you are taking looks from the outside. Give your close connections time to get used to the you that emerges from each leg of the adventure. Let them know in every way you can that the changes they see in style or pace or preferences are not about loving or respecting them less, but rather about knowing and caring better for yourself. When you make a life that has more integrity and is lived more intentionally, no one loses. And the more willing you are to communicate your intentions, the easier it will be for your close connections to perceive the mutual gain and lay their fears to rest.

If you sense that someone you care about is troubled over the changes you're making, seek some simple way to express your love and remind them of their place in your life.

- *Make a special one-on-one date. (This works with friends, lovers, parents and children — even bosses!)*
- *Send a note of appreciation or a small, thoughtful gift that says, "You're important to me."*
- *Make a quick, one-subject phone call to say, "I just wanted you to know that I was thinking about you."*

Talk about what you're up to and how it is moving you in the direction you need and want to go. Show your own enthusiasm and talk about the specific ways in which you are happier. Let them know that their feelings about it are important to you, because you want them to be as happy as you are.

Share the adventure.

No one ever said that simplifying life is a one-person show. In fact, if you try to redesign your life in relation to others without their knowledge or involvement, you will almost certainly run smack into a very thick, painfully immovable wall. You have to begin with yourself, but you cannot end there. The other people in your life appropriately expect to be included in the plans and changes you make that affect them. If you actively draw others into your hopes and plans, you will be easing the way toward making your relational life an exciting and positive part of your life. You may be surprised at how enthusiastic family and friends can be when you broach the subject of simplifying. After all, you aren't the only one who is feeling overwhelmed and underfulfilled.

The closer you are to another person, the more you can seek to involve them in the positive changes you hope to make. In some cases, making the simplifying process a mutual project can add a dimension to a particular relationship you never dreamed possible. And it can transform the dynamic of a group.

Expect some intermediate complications.

It often takes a series of changes to reach the end result we want. To reach a simpler life, we may first have to endure new, added complications, especially as our changes affect others.

Choose at least one of the changes you hope to make and consider the impact it will have on you and on others. Institute the Powwow Principle (see page 74) to talk out with others the decisions that affect them. Remember that solutions never come in either-or packages. There is always at least one other option and often many others. The more imaginations that are put to work on problem solving, the more likely you are to come up with solutions that everyone can live with.

A wife and mom goes back to school

When Jody returned to school as an adult wife and mother of four, her immediate family supported her — in theory. She had a strong natural talent in the visual arts, but she felt frustrated by what she didn't know and the limitations it put on what she could produce as an artist. She had waited through her husband's extended education and through the early years of her last-born child. Everyone seemed to agree that it was her turn.

But they didn't reckon with the changes in home life Jody's education would necessitate. Nor did they anticipate the external, negative pressure that would come from extended family. Jody had been the ultimate homemaker, providing plenty of artistic and homegrown, homemade attention, meals, chauffeuring, entertaining, decorating and gifts. She ran her home and family life like a very successful business, with herself in the role of owner/operator. She was always available, always up to the minute on the needs and desires of five other people and their various networks.

"The first year was bad," she says now. "We were one cranky bunch of people. The house was grubby, the meals were rushed, the kids didn't always have the exact item of clothing that they needed clean, we missed appointments. My husband and my parents, even my own sister, began to make comments that left me feeling selfish and alone."

Finally, in the middle of a pitched battle one Sunday afternoon, Jody called a truce. She asked everyone to sit around the kitchen table. She handed out pieces of paper and asked everyone to write down what they wanted that they weren't getting because she was in school. They then took turns reading what they had written. When it was Jody's turn, she read her list — one single item: "Your help."

It launched a new way of working the home scene. The family collaborated to make a master sheet of the jobs and issues. They figured out a reasonable way to divvy up the work so that everyone was involved. "We still have our problems," Jody says. "But we're in it together. I've become more dispensable, and Jack and the kids" — said with a smile — "have learned some valuable life skills. I have actually heard them bragging about what they do around here."

You've assesssed who and where you are in relation to others. You've begun to prepare yourself for the effects of change. It still remains to put yourself and your intentions into action. Each kind of relationship — mate, family, friend and community — has its unique challenges. Plan ahead for the challenges and rewards of change. Then take the steps that will rebuild your connections to others to suit the kind of future you want.

Reinventing family life

A family may be two people or it may be ten. It may exist under one roof, extend over geography and time to include an entire clan, or comprise a group blended together from previous family groups. Regardless of the makeup of your family, you're in good company if you're feeling the complexities of family life in the modern world. Take courage! You can find some helpful ways to sort out and simplify the dynamics of living together.

Institute a regular meeting.

Base your family meeting on the Powwow Principle (see page 74) and make it weekly or monthly. Schedule it for a time when you can reasonably expect everyone to be available and involved.

The week before your powwow, post a sheet of lined paper on the refrigerator. Anyone who has an item for discussion can write it on the sheet of paper, which will then serve as that meeting's agenda.

Rotate the responsibility for chairing the meeting. A young child (up to age five) will need the help of an older sibling or parent, but any child who is school age is old enough to hold the gavel. Even if your family is simply a pair of adults, this is a great tool for simplifying your life together.

TO SIMPLIFY FAMILY

Institute a regular meeting.

Focus on people.

Simplify together time.

Share the work.

Make plans together.

Give everyone room.

Focus on people.

For most people, family life has long since evolved from a centralized world of shared activity to a wild, confusing list of individual activities that turn any drivers in the family into chauffeurs and make any together time rare. We all cry over lost "quality time." But one of the reasons why it's lost is because we throw away the opportunities that still exist to pay attention to each other. (For instance, consider how many families spend most of their shared time staring at a TV.) Think about the times you have with family. Notice how often you actually look others in the eye. Observe how much time you spend listening. What steps can you take to shift the focus of that time to noticing and appreciating the people you are with?

The Powwow Principle

We take the idea of the powwow — a meeting that draws members of a community together for discussion or celebration — from a long-standing Native North American tradition. At its heart is the emphasis on mutual care and support. Its practice allows people in today's fragmented family lifestyle to build wholeness together. A few simple rules:

- **Work as a team.** Every discussion should aim for a resolution that everyone can agree to. Include time to praise one another — for achievements, good deeds, generosity and any other items that deserve a simple "I love who you are."
- **Develop common goals** (for example, fair distribution of housework, privacy for all family members, time together, family-planned fun). This should be done as a group and recorded.
- **Avoid accusation.** If conflict needs to be resolved, practice "When that happens, I feel" language rather than "You make me feel . . ."
- **Use the plus-minus quotient.** For every negative statement someone makes, they must find something positive to say.
- **Make the powwow a high priority, but be flexible.** Decide together what counts as a legitimate reason for rescheduling (a school event, illness, out-of-town guests, unavoidable out-of-town business) and what does not (social plans, another meeting, television, a phone call).
- **Let any family member call a special meeting.** The Powwow Principle works because it builds an atmosphere of collaboration, trust and communication. If one member of the family has a problem, the whole family has a problem. So be ready to respond if someone asks for talk time.

Simplify together time.

We sometimes have trouble focusing on the people in our family because we let the business of family — meals, housework, logistics — overtake us. Consider whether you've overestimated the value of some of that business to the point that it's getting in the way of good people time. If, for example, you're of the elaborate-dinners persuasion — what Russell Baker once called the "Pile-It-On" school of cooking — think about cutting the number of fancy meals down. Look around for cookbooks that offer recipes for "Meals in a Minute" (you won't have to look far), "One-dish Cooking," "Salad Suppers" and other low-fuss food.

As you simplify the cooking and cleanup, you'll have more energy, time and attention for the people at the table and for other ways of being together. The same principle can be applied to any facet of family business. Take none of your family "work" for granted. Look for ways that you can trim, tailor and eliminate the work that doesn't add lasting value.

Share the work.

No matter how much simpler you make your life over time, you'll always have "home" work that needs doing to keep a household running well. You can make shared life simpler by making sure that the work of home is part of what you share among all the members of your family. Children need to be trained to take responsibility for some part of the work, and they need to be held accountable for their share. Adult members of a family will share the work best if they agree ahead of time about who is responsible for what. Invest the time needed to plan how family work will be done and by whom. It's worth it.

Make plans together.

Fun has become big business. Vacations, recreation, meals out and special events can be complicated and expensive, and they are sometimes so elaborate that families finish their "time off" together feeling as though they need another break just to recover. Add to that the stress of spending (and sometimes overspending), and vacations become a burden instead of the recreation and relaxation they're intended to be. But alternatives to high-ticket, high-tension fun can be had for the cost of some thought and a little imagination. Try one or more of these ideas.

• *Create your wish list.* Discuss as a family what matters most to you when you're having fun. Is it the break from the normal routine? Spending time as a family? Physical activity, reading or sitting in the sun? Give some reflection time to the idea of time off before you make solid plans for your next breather.

• *Call a family powwow* to come up with at least five day trips that cost nothing and add one or more of the elements that are important to you. Try a hike, a picnic, a softball game with another

A single-parent family

John is a single dad who was finding it difficult to keep up with all the work associated with dinners. He finally hit on a method that has taken the dread and weariness out of the job.

First, John made a master list on his computer of food items he uses. Next he collected quick-and-easy recipes that would suit his children's tastes, make at least enough for two meals and freeze well. Finally, he involved the children in all stages of the work.

Together they choose the week's menus from John's recipe card file. They check off all the food items on the master list they will need to purchase. John shops when the children can go along, and they divide the list, each child equipped with a handbasket. John functions as "shopping-cart central." At home the children rotate as chef's helper and cleanup crew, and the oldest now takes his turns as chef-in-charge.

"It took some work in the beginning," John admits. "But I've gotten to know my kids so much better since we started this. We have more time together, and we talk about all kinds of things as we work."

family, a Ping-Pong tournament or a board game marathon. Visit a beautiful spot with nothing but a packed lunch and a Frisbee.

• *Make a "Places to Go" book.* Keep a notebook or folder handy for recreation planning. Every time any family member hears or reads about an interesting free event, place or activity, write it in the notebook or clip it and glue it in. Refer to it when you're ready to relax as a family. This brainstorm-in-a-book can work for more extended getaways as well, and it can give you ideas for time alone.

• *Take an unvacation.* Use some time off to luxuriate in the *lack* of plans. Read a book together. Play games. Do a jigsaw puzzle. Make taffy or fudge or some other forbidden treat that takes a lot of hands. The possibilities are limitless, given love and imagination.

• *Declare one day a week "recharge day."* The fact that stores are open seven days a week, often 24 hours a day, doesn't have to dictate the way you live your life. Take advantage of the week's cycle by marking the week's beginning with a day that's different from the rest. Take a break from shopping, work, paying bills, finishing projects. Give yourself and each other permission to do something completely out of the ordinary or to do nothing at all. It sounds obvious, but how many of us do it?

• *Declare every sixth weekend a vacation.* If you plan ahead, you can make your own time off. Don't fall into the rut of thinking that vacations come only in weeklong increments once or twice a year. And don't shackle yourself to the idea that you have to wait until you have no outstanding work in the in-basket. Never fear! Home care will wait for you. Business needs to be neglected occasionally or it takes over. Almost all deadlines can be nudged a day or two. In fact, people who practice planned play report that they get more done, not less. And some of the "to do's" that eat up relaxation time are not nearly as crucial as you think.

Give everyone room.

A room of one's own is great. But even more important is heart space. One of the fundamental keys to making life together simpler is nurturing time apart. In *The Road Less Traveled,* Scott Peck includes in his definition of love the idea of separateness. "A major characteristic of genuine love," he says, "is that the distinction between oneself and the other is always maintained and preserved." How do we maintain this distinction? By freely, sympathetically allowing one another to have time and space alone, to pursue relationships and activities outside of the family as well as in, and sometimes to choose a separate path.

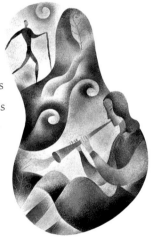

Mining the gold in friendships

"A friend may well be reckoned the masterpiece of Nature," wrote Ralph Waldo Emerson, in his essays on friendship. Recently, a medical doctor, on hearing about my habit of walking daily with a close friend, told me, "If more people did what you're doing, I'd have more free time!" — and he wasn't referring to the exercise.

Friendship may be one of the richest gifts of life, but it sometimes also weighs us down with the complications it adds to our lives. Why? Because we move from care for one another to what Christiane Northrup, of the University of Vermont School of Medicine, calls "overcare." "Whenever caring for your family, your job or any aspect of your life gives you more stress and heartache than pleasure and joy," writes Dr. Northrup, "you can be sure that you are participating in overcare."

TO UNCOMPLICATE FRIENDSHIP

Know your limits.

Communicate simply.

Manage the telephone.

Simplify gifts.

Simplify gatherings.

Friendships fall into the overcare category when we fail to set realistic boundaries within them (about time, money, emotional dependence or other commitments). We suffer from overcare when we slip into habits of dishonesty (about what we want or need, how we feel, or what we can actually offer). So too when we try to "fix" other people's problems (assuming too much responsibility) or ask other people to fix ours (relinquishing responsibility, falling into unhealthy dependencies).

All of the overcare areas grow out of potentially positive aspects of friendship. As you become aware of what needs to be simplified, you can focus on building up the best parts of friendship and make choices that transform overcaring into healthy affection.

Know your limits.

We can't be everyone's friend. Every friendship represents a commitment of time and attention, and each of us has only so much time and attention to give. With this in mind:

• *Start slowly.* Think as much about the level of a new friendship as you would about a new job or a promise of money.

• *Look at the quality of the time you spend together.* Are you just logging hours? Avoid some abstract ideal of "being together."

• *Practice "less-is-more" planning.* Make the most of the time you have together, then build more breathing room between visits.

• *Avoid standing dates.* Make times together a free choice every time, and be honest when you don't have the time.

Communicate simply.

Drop a line — just one! Buy in a supply of note cards or postcards that have a minimum of writing space. Keep them, with postage stamps, in a convenient spot. When you think of someone special, want to say thanks or just want to connect, write a quick note (don't make a project of it — a few short lines at most) and pop it in the mail the same day.

Manage the telephone.

Two of my closest friends have moved far enough away that the phone has become a lifeline of communication. But we have all felt the bite into our phone budgets, and being forced by cost to watch the length of phone calls has taught us an important lesson. Longer is not necessarily better. In fact, as much as we love our friends, we don't always welcome the phone calls that go on for hours.

- *Call when you have only ten minutes before you have to leave the house for an appointment.*
- *Jot down what you want to talk about before you call.*
- *Unplug the phone when you would rather not talk.*
- *Give friends "calling hours." "I'm no good after 8:00 P.M."*
  or "I'm not available before 9:30 A.M." or "Not tomorrow."

When you take control of this valuable tool, you'll be able to use it as a simplifier instead of being ruled by it.

Simplify gifts.

As our circle of friends grows, we sometimes find ourselves with a nerve-racking list of birthdays, holidays and special occasions to remember. This is where some gentle honesty is indispensable. First of all, you should feel free to decide whether or not you want to exchange gifts at all. If gift giving appeals, here are some ideas to get your generosity fueled in new directions.

- *Agree together and ahead of time to scale back.* You should feel free to say, "Gifts have gotten to be more of a chore than a pleasure. Let's try something different." Then suggest a theme or a limit: "something smaller than a wallet," "something for the beach" or "something that costs less than $10." Work on the idea together.

• *Make a mutual outing your yearly gift to one another.* Focus on common interests. Do you love sports? Decide to buy tickets to the game of choice together. Are you art fans? Watch for an exhibit that appeals to you both and make a date to see it.

• *Share something you own that has been special to you.* On several occasions, I have received gifts of used books or music with a personalized note that explained what it had meant to my friend and why it seemed "right" for me. Far from feeling cheated, I appreciated the shared "vocabulary" the gift gave us, and I cherished the adventure into someone else's private world.

• *Give consumables.* Try specialty soaps; a basket filled with the nonperishable ingredients for an ethnic meal; a flowering plant; a collection of dried herbs; golf balls and tees; a blank book; tickets to a show; or a gift certificate to a fancy restaurant or specialty shop.

• *Give a charitable gift on behalf of your friend.* A friend of mine began to use the money that he might have spent on obligatory gifts (birthdays, holidays, anniversaries) to help supply a local shelter. Each time, he would send a note to the friend whose special day had precipitated the gift, to let them know that his love for them had been expressed in a charitable way. Eventually, he and a number of those friends made a trip together to the shelter, which led to their volunteering together as occasional helpers.

• *Plant a tree.* This can be a lifelong gift that symbolizes the deepening nature of friendship. Choose a spot that has special significance to you both, or make a ritual of the planting itself.

• *Give when it's not expected.* Instead of meeting all the obligatory dates, it can be refreshing to give a gift to a friend for no reason other than to say "I care about you." An ungift may be the most appreciated gift you'll ever give, and it comes with no expectations, so it can be the simplest of gifts as well.

Friendship is a gift. Taking the time and making the effort to simplify the way you carry on your friendships will allow you to enjoy your friends all the more.

Simplify gatherings.

Holidays and entertaining can highlight relationships and create memories we carry with us for a lifetime. They can also leave us drained and anxious, in debt, or depressed. If social events have become a burden in your life, it's probably time to consider whether your motives for throwing or attending group get-togethers match who you are and what you value most.

Ask yourself whether the good reasons you have for group get-togethers are being served by the events in which you now participate. Explore alternatives that will bring the events and your values more in sync. Great ideas proliferate for simpler parties and holidays. Try any of these to tip the scale from stress to pleasure:

• *Skip the all-family holiday.* So many people bring emotional baggage to family holidays, it's a wonder we still celebrate these occasions. But there's no law of nature that says we have to spend the special day with the extended family. If what you really want is to let family members know that you love them, find other times that don't carry the same psycho-freight to gather with them, or join only smaller parts of the whole gang at a time. Make the holiday itself a time for the nuclear family, for friends and acquaintances who have nowhere to go, or for visiting shut-ins, soup kitchens, the hospital or a prison.

• *Shift to reduced gift exchanges.* Traditional gift exchanges become monstrous when you're buying for 25-plus individuals in your family. The same can happen among large groups of friends who have "traditional" annual parties. Try passing a hat of names among any groups that customarily exchange gifts so that everyone can give to just one other person and receive from one. It's still fun and much less complicated.

• *Throw an everyone-helps theme party.* This is a twist on the old standard, the potluck (still a perfectly good idea as well). Choose a central motif (season of the year, region of the country, foreign country, off-the-beaten-track holiday, good news, music or art style, historical era, literature). Let each guest contribute part of the food, beverage, music or decoration, all taken from the theme.

• *Give a make-it-yourself dinner.* Plan a dinner party that allows each guest to participate in the process of making the meal. Any soup or stew works well (all that chopping, sautéing and stirring keeps many hands busy). Pizza, burritos, fondue, tempura, main-dish salads and sundaes allow for creative, custom-designed offerings that people can make for themselves or for trade.

• *Invite friends for brunch, appetizers or dessert.* In the Netherlands, people usually gather for coffee and cookies, rather than a full-course dinner. We've recently moved to a village where one extended family always follows the Memorial Day parade with pots of coffee and boxed doughnuts for their large extended family and any friends family members want to invite (we were invited and we had a blast). Brunch or appetizers — if you don't get carried away — can be a simple, inexpensive alternative to the more elaborate dinner party.

Contributing to the community

We live not only in our families and among our friends. We also participate in the larger society that frames our personal lives. Community life often calls for individual involvement, whether in government, local leadership, jury duty, cooperative associations, clubs, special interest groups, cultural events, charitable organizations or community projects. Sometimes our involvement is our part- or full-time work. More often it is a volunteer effort. Such local organizations as churches, PTAs, public libraries, garden clubs, soup kitchens, Meals on Wheels, literacy programs and fire departments depend on regular folks to help keep the wheels of community life turning. At the national and international level, the Peace Corps, Red Cross, Habitat for Humanity and other service organizations ask volunteers to offer time, skills and compassion to make a better world.

Regardless of your level of involvement with community — whether it is paid for, obligatory or volunteer; international, national or local — the work is meaningful, the needs great. Many people derive some of their deepest satisfaction in life in community work.

Sometimes, however, community involvement becomes a burden, part of what keeps us overworked and out of sorts. Anyone who has contributed much community time knows how it works. Ten percent (at best) of those involved end up giving 90 percent of the effort. We become resentful. We burn out. In the midst of our good work, we grumble, "Nobody's paying me for this, y'know!" or "I'm not paid enough for this aggravation!" Eventually, we may even lose our desire to contribute at all.

TO SIMPLIFY INVOLVEMENT

Do one job well.

Limit your commitment.

Cultivate one other community recruit.

Take a sabbatical.

The truth is, you have an unusual level of control over the level and quality of your involvement in community — how much you agree to do in the first place, and how far above and beyond the call of duty and/or generosity you rise. If you put in place some simple and sane principles for reasonable community activity, you can happily reclaim the satisfactions and meaning that come with the work.

Do one job well.

Gifted people are sometimes tempted to do everything because they do it better than others. Energetic people often jump in to fill a need for fear that no one else will. In both cases, an important element of community life is lost. Younger, shier, less gifted or less experienced people never have the chance to grow and contribute as long as the supercompetent few continue to plug themselves into every empty slot. Try limiting yourself to one job at a time. Find the job that you can invest your passion in. You'll still be contributing, enjoy yourself more and make room for others to join in the meaningful work of serving others.

Limit your commitment.

If the volunteer position doesn't come with a term limit, create one. It's important for everyone (including you) that continuing is a free, current choice. A reasonable time before your term expires,

A
volunteer
who is too
good

Donna is an imaginative, energetic woman who for years readily volunteered for her church's annual bazaar. Every year, her co-volunteers noticed more of her abilities. To her first job of soliciting raffle contributions from local vendors, they encouraged her to add running the bake sale, planning the booths, handling the bookkeeping and, eventually, chairing the promotion committee.

That was the year the proverbial straw landed on the camel's back. For weeks, Donna's days were tinged with frustration and panic. She was saddled with more than one person could handle, but she agreed to each added task because it was for a good cause. In the final analysis, her whole pack of "Yes's" overloaded her.

Donna wised up, but the changes did not come easily. People had gotten used to her hypercontributions. When she informed the steering committee that she had decided to do just one job, the dismay was universal and immediate. For the first year of her limited involvement, it looked as though some of the jobs wouldn't be done. Eventually, though, the "right" volunteer appeared for every job.

consider whether you want to continue what you're doing. Be sure to give your coworkers ample notice if you choose to stop. Otherwise, you may (appropriately) feel that you're leaving them in the lurch if they have trouble finding a replacement.

Cultivate one other community recruit.

Watch for the hidden talents in others. Some people are easy to overlook because they never draw attention to themselves. That doesn't mean that they don't have something to offer, or that they don't want a chance to offer it. Keep your eyes open for the shy ones who stand on the sidelines. Pay attention to younger people (including adolescents) who may never have had an invitation or opportunity to be involved. Make it your goal to encourage one other person to be part of a worthy work. You'll be helping them and broadening the base of potential helpers.

Take a sabbatical.

We all need periodic rests if we're going to be enthusiastic participants in community life. We also need to know that we're dispensable if we're going to serve others cheerfully, understanding that our contribution is a free gift, not an unwanted obligation. And we need to stand back, applaud and support the good work of others if we're going to maintain a spirit of humility. Take a break with a clear conscience.

Remember that many of the complications that grow in our relationships are not nearly as large or problematic as we believe them to be. A wise friend once told me that we teach people how to be our friends. That could as easily read "how to be our children/parents/coworkers/neighbors." If we learn to know and respect ourselves and our values, we have the psychological fitness to demonstrate to others how best we can relate. We can begin to toss the extra baggage of so-called obligations and expectations that we have allowed others to associate with us. We can build new habits that help to enhance good relationships and repair needy ones. We may even find that some people and their demands simply don't fit in our lives. We've bogged down because we kept taking on people the way we do shoes or groceries.

Relational life is intrinsically complicated, and relationships are often messy, but we can learn new ways to live intentionally with others that are more appropriate to what we hope for in life. On the other side of the simplifying effort come greater personal peace and satisfaction, more honest relationships, and community involvement that we can delight in. Let togetherness become the centerpiece of a simpler, better life.

Home Simple Home

"*Everyone has, I think, in some quiet corner of his mind, an ideal home waiting to become a reality,*" *writes Paige Rense, editor-in-chief of* Architectural Digest.

What is the ideal home? Is it the perfect floor plan? The most beautiful furnishings? Location, location, location? Any or all of these elements may contribute to the ideal home, but they will ultimately let us down unless they serve our deepest needs. A simpler life requires a simpler home, a place that matches our spirit, our style and our needs.

Let's talk about home. The first definition of *home* in the dictionary is "a place of residence." True, but insufficient. Second is "the social unit formed by a family living together." That's more like it. It has the ring of "Home is where the heart is," the long-lasting aphorism of a good ol' boy from the Roman Empire named Pliny. It puts a lot of single people in the category of homeless, however, so let's move on to my personal favorite. It's a single word: "habitat." That seems just about right to me. It includes all sorts of living arrangements. It calls up visions of an environment or an ecosystem, a place that's dynamic and organic, located somewhere on the line between domesticated and wild, inhabited by a loose and changing collection of people, animals, dust bunnies and debris — in short, a typical home.

The average home manager is no longer defined solely as a female. S/he must juggle people, pets, possessions, property maintenance, plumbing, electricity, laundry, cleaning, food planning and preparation, dry rot and mildew, entertaining, and such business as bills, phone and mail. I don't believe there has ever been a time as materialistic or frenetic as the present. We own more, consume more, travel more, aspire to more and demand more on a global scale than in any other era in history. All that "more" has to reside somewhere. Quite a lot of it lives with us in our homes. The resulting bulge-at-the-seams home environment we live in makes the entire home enterprise seem overwhelming.

Books have been written on how to sell all, how to abandon our high-cost, high-tech, overlarge living spaces and get back to the basics. Let's take it as a given that most of us don't really want to go to that extreme. We just want to get it under control. We want a reasonably clean, comfortable, life-enhancing habitat that we can manage in our spare time, open to friends without embarrassment and snuggle into at the end of a workday or workweek. The good news is, it's attainable. You don't have to sell the ranch or make a clean sweep of all your belongings.

A simpler home, in essence, is one that contains only what you need and like. It is easy to clean and to maintain. And it is decorated and arranged to promote your rest and refreshment, peace and well-being. If you focus on these areas with simplifying in mind, you can start making the changes that will create a simpler, more satisfying home.

The first and most obvious step requires a long, hard look at all our collection areas. We need to sift out the overload — both the visible mess and the chaos tucked away in all those modern storage areas we insist on having. Imagine a home without drawers you can't open because they're so full; without mystery stashes in corners, behind doors and under beds; without so many items on every available surface that dusting has become a juggling act. Do

you really need those twist-ties? When did you last use the
automatic potato slicer? How about that wool jacket with the coffee
stain and the ripped lining? Or the orphan socks, mittens, earrings
and cuff links? Or the obsolete chain saw? Or the million and one
spare nuts and bolts? Or the extra furniture in a small room?

An honest assessment of your belongings allows you to
decide what you really want and need in your home. And a little
effort and imagination applied to what you no longer want frees
you of that extra baggage. But paring down your belongings is only
part of simplifying home. You also need to simplify the
maintenance of what's left. Inefficiencies build over time, as you
add activities, people, things or pets without dealing consciously
with the impact any of them have on what is already there. When
you've trimmed your home of extras, it's easy to develop (or return
to) simpler maintenance routines that keep your home open and
clean, restful, and in good repair without undue toil. The bonus is
time and space to make your home a place that fits and pleases you.

Making home leaner

The comedian Steven Wright says it best: "You can't have
everything. Where would you put it?" Unfortunately, many of us
forget the fundamental wisdom beneath his humor. We act as if
we *can* have everything, and *ought* to. Before we know it, we need

A change of address unearths the truth

My family and I recently moved from a 2,400-square-foot house. One of its greatest virtues was that it had a place for everything. Everything we owned fit, without cluttering up our living space.

But when we began to unload all the "places" that held "everything," we discovered that behind the tidy facade, we had accumulated heaps of unused, forgotten, broken or outgrown "stuff." My son assures me that matter can be neither created nor destroyed. I beg to differ. I'd swear I'd never seen half the items in those piles of clothes, decorations, appliances and pieces of furniture. One thing was certain. We could not move it all.

Thus began a monumental — and revealing — sorting project that led not only to worthy donations, a bonfire and some nifty pickings for the folks at the dump but to the family's reassessment of what we really need and want to carry with us, literally in the move and metaphorically throughout life.

More than a year later, I can't remember what we got rid of, but I can tell you this. We haven't missed a thing.

a garage, attic, basement and toolshed to hold all the machines, out-of-season goods, furniture, old and new bicycles, and exotic appliances. We need closets, bureaus and bookcases to contain the clothes, dishes, supplies, books and toys we keep.

You've probably heard the expression "Time is money." What you don't hear, but should, is that space is money too. Every square foot we use costs us in rent or mortgage, taxes, upkeep, furnishings, security systems and effort. We want to simplify. We wish we didn't have to work so hard to earn enough money to afford our home, to keep up with cleaning, property care, replacing the obsolete. But because we have bought the consumer version of the good life, our accumulated material goods are closing in on us. Instead of us owning them, they are beginning to own us.

It's time to start un-"stuff"-ing the storage. Overload is not hopeless. If you routinely unstuff in logical stages — sorting, shucking and storing — you can permanently let light, air and freedom into the storage spaces in your life.

Sort out storage areas.

You have to start somewhere, and as in other areas of simplifying, I'm a great advocate of feeling the pain and starting there. What's the first place, pile or stash that came to your mind as you read the paragraphs above? That's probably your greatest point of pain. Why not let that area be your trial run on the unstuff trail?

• *Start small.* Don't take on the whole garage, the entire basement or attic. Don't even expect to do a whole closet. Choose one corner of a storage room, the floor under the bed, the shelf in the hall closet, the drawer by the back door. Decide how much time you want to devote to sorting — it can be 15 minutes or two days, whatever you can realistically afford or sustain. I can't emphasize this enough. A vital part of simplifying is learning to manage and enjoy the *process.* Bite off only as much as you know you can finish in your chosen amount of time. When the time is up and the job, however small, is finished, treat yourself to a walk, a good book, a half hour on the driving range, or a visit with a neighbor or friend. You deserve a pat on the back. You've started!

• *Grab some containers and a permanent marker.* However small the problem space, it has reached its present mess because it needs sorting. You'll make the sorting process 100 percent easier by sorting directly into containers.

TO PARE DOWN TO "JUST RIGHT"

Sort out storage areas.

Shuck the excess.

Store the keepers.

Start with a good supply of industrial-strength trash bags. Assume at the outset that some of what you are sorting has become trash since you last stowed it. Next in line, and just as important, are smaller bags (grocery bags are easy to come by and good to get rid of) or boxes that you can label and load up with different categories of keepables. Before you begin, label one "To Pass Along." The rest of the bags you can label

according to what you find: "Kitchen," "Cleaning," "For Uncle
Hank," "Holiday decorations," "Vacation games" and so on.

• *Allocate the space.* Once you've removed the contents of
the space you're sorting, decide what that space is best used for. If
it's part of a much larger space — the attic, for example — you may
not be ready to do so. In that case, let it become the *temporary*
storage place for your *temporary* containers of sorted goods. This
does *not* include the trash bags. They go. Today. Now.

If you've emptied a complete space — say, a shelf in a closet
or a drawer in the den — decide now what you want to store in
that place. Make sure it's logical. If you want a place to put the
remote control, *TV Guide,* coasters and cocktail napkins, some pens
and your crossword puzzle book, all of which you use in the den,
then the den drawer is perfect for those items. Put only what you've
planned in the space you've allocated. All other items are now
trashed, or sorted and placed in *temporary* storage. (I hope you're
noticing the emphasis on *temporary*. You might as well not start if
you're only going to shuffle the mess.)

• *Start again.* Good job! Now that you've had your first
taste of the sorting process, it's time to move on. Choose the next
spot and plan a time to tackle it. The point is, keep whittling away
at the job of unstuffing, bit by bit. The image of whittling should
help you think about what you're doing. You just keep paring off
the excess, reducing the size and shaping what remains until you

have a quiet, harmonious storage environment that serves your needs and suits your spirit.

Shuck the excess.

Once you're well into the sorting process, you will have an accumulation of goods that no longer belong in your home. Faster is better for trash disposal, lest you remember the old (bad) reasons you kept some of those items in the first place and dig them out again. Make recycling a weekly habit, as automatic as brushing your teeth. Enormous amounts of space are lost to recyclables that have stopped cycling.

For the rest of the misfits, the range of possibilities will depend on what they are, who you are, whom you know, where you live and how much work you want to invest in disposing of non-trash items. Think in terms of what you can give away and what you might want to sell. Either way, you're contributing to the worldwide effort of making less trash.

• *Hand-me-downs.* Sharing with others what we no longer need or use is an old-fashioned notion that still works. Maternity and infant clothes and furniture are obvious — these items don't have time to wear out before they lose their relevance to our own lives. But they barely scratch the surface of the possible hand-alongs that take up space in our homes.

Be on the lookout for folks who would welcome a cheap or free source of used appliances and tools, serviceable utensils, dishes, linens, lamps and furniture, replaced curtains and rugs, the old Weber grill, and the outgrown bicycles. Tune in to college students, young people setting up housekeeping for the first time, single parents and others who suddenly have to start fresh on a slim budget, or newcomers to the country. If you feel awkward offering your used items, ask a general question in the context of a friendly conversation: "Would you have any interest in or use for . . . It's still in good condition and I hate to throw it away." That way, you don't risk insulting anyone or burdening them with something they don't want. More important, you allow them their dignity.

• *Donations.* Always remember charity. There are so many people all around us who struggle just to have the basics. And the outlets for donating a whole range of goods proliferate. Because they vary from place to place, finding the right place for your used items may take a little investigation, but it will pay heartwarming dividends in the ongoing process of simplifying your home.

Many towns have a collection box for the Salvation Army that takes clothes and shoes, and the organization also runs a free pickup service for furniture and boxes of used appliances. Goodwill also collects usable goods. Both services refurbish and sell the items at a discount. The proceeds keep the charitable organization running, and provide jobs for disadvantaged people.

A friend's "extras" meet a need

Kim decorated solely with handed-down furnishings for the first 20 years of her adult life, redeeming old pieces with a good stripping and a coat of paint or varnish, slipcovers, or simple add-ons. She has kept some of those pieces because they now have such unique character and charm that she can't imagine finding something new that would compare. She didn't love *all* the hand-me-downs, however. She'd inherited a pair of Early American loveseats that she faithfully revamped for color and wear, but she couldn't change the fact that they were too small to be comfortable for family use and too "Early American" to suit her style.

About the time she could afford to replace them with something more to her liking, a young, newly married friend mentioned how much she loved those loveseats. Kim explained that the foam rubber in the cushions was turning to dust and that the slipcovers were beginning to fade. Her friend responded that she would be thrilled to have them. She and her new husband had an apartment, but no furniture. *Voilà!* Two fewer unwanted items in Kim's home. Two happy people.

Contact your local churches or synagogues to see if they have a system for passing along used items to people in need. Be sure to ask what kind of items they take and what condition the items need to be in. Many churches have an outlet for used eyeglasses, so check that out as well.

Call your town hall to find out if your town runs a clothing bank. Many towns and regional businesses operate a winter clothing drop, where people can donate their castoff coats, snowsuits, scarves, gloves, mittens and blankets for the needy.

If you live in a town in which homeless shelters, social services and soup kitchens exist, you may find that some of your hand-alongs will be welcome there.

Don't forget your local schools. Old computers, craft supplies, certain recyclables, out-of-date clothing, even old furniture may be welcome donations to computer or science labs, the drama club, a kindergarten supply closet, or student lounge.

• *Goods for sale.* You may want or need to capitalize on your efforts to simplify by selling some of what you no longer wish to keep. You can slim down your belongings for profit in a variety of ways, depending again on the time or effort you want to invest.

Whether you call it a yard sale, garage sale or tag sale, it's a modern institution. Collect your unwanted items, buy a supply of tiny stick-on tags, price the items (most experienced salers say it's best to keep small items under a dollar; furniture is another matter) and choose a day to put the marked items outside your house. Some neighborhoods hold a "block sale" in a cul-de-sac.

Another option that will suit apartment dwellers better is an ad in the local paper or swap rag. Local talk-radio stations sometimes conduct tag sales on the air, and listeners are invited to call in and describe their sale items on the air. Laundromats and community cafés often have bulletin boards on which people can post items for sale. Simply type up a description and add your phone number (include times to call, if you want).

You can also look for a consignment shop that accepts used items for sale. You need to decide how much money you want for your goods; the shop owner will add a percentage onto that for the shop. This is a good option if you dislike the wheeling and dealing, but you may earn less than you could, and your items may not be displayed to advantage.

If you suspect that some of the items you want to get rid of could have substantial value, ask around about reputable antique or used-furniture dealers who can advise you on pricing and may even buy your items themselves. One way or another, you can continue to pass along all those belongings that just don't belong anymore and move further along the path to simpler living.

Store the keepers.

It's impossible to talk about simplifying storage without reciting the old adage "A place for everything and everything in its place." If you don't have and can't make a place for something in your home, then it doesn't belong there. If you want or need something, it's worth the effort of finding a suitable place for it. Many books are available on how to maximize storage space, if you need some ideas. Pursue a couple of basic storage principles, and you'll be amazed at how much simpler life becomes.

• *Apply logic.* The top of your refrigerator is a "place." But if you decide to store your tennis shoes there, you will have introduced an extraneous item into the kitchen and undermined the confidence of your friends and family in your hygiene. When you're looking for the place to put something or allocating a recently redeemed storage area, pay attention to what makes sense.

Store items as close to where they are used as possible. Keep like items together. (Create storage centers for cleaning and gardening tools and supplies, out-of-season clothing that needs pest protection, automotive care, sports equipment, books, toys, sewing, crafts and hobbies, and home maintenance and repair.) And store backup consumables where they are readily visible and accessible. Otherwise, you may find yourself storing far more backup items than you need or, worse, keeping the excess items so long that they become trash.

An opportunity to make a simple sale

On the death of his only surviving parent, Bob inherited a load of heavy Victorian furniture. He held onto it for years because it held sentimental value, even though it didn't suit him and was too large for his living space. Eventually, however, the furniture came to feel like an anchor around his neck.

Bob lived across the street from a small church. Every Sunday, people would park all along his street, including in front of his house. One Sunday, in a sudden courageous burst of determination, Bob dragged the big, old, velvet-covered sofa that was part of his inheritance out onto his lawn and propped a sign on it that read: "For sale. Best offer." Ten minutes after the Sunday service let out, he had three people bidding to buy that sofa. When people heard that he had more furniture in that style available, they begged him to let them buy. With the proceeds, Bob carefully bought simpler, smaller furnishings that have made his house much more the home he wants it to be.

- *Use containers.* Some useful and needed items are by
nature a mess. You can take control of all sorts of items — pens and
pencils, nuts and bolts, mending supplies, assorted underwear,
paper napkins, tennis balls, catalogs — and make your storage
more efficient by stowing them in right-size, well-marked
containers. Use *recycled containers in mint condition* (shoe boxes, egg
cartons, shipping cartons, plastic tubs from packaged products);
purchased containers (Rubbermaid, Tupperware and other hard-
sided containers — buy them only as you need them); or *handmade
containers* (if you're handy, construct wooden boxes or sew up cloth
drawstring bags that suit exactly your space and storables).

Remember: Once you've contained your keepables, put
them in a place that makes sense for them to be.

Your simplifying should never wander from the original
assessments you have made. This is all about who you are, and
whom and what you value most in life. Every item you have chosen
to keep should fit. Ask again: Do I need/want/have space or use for
this item? If you answer "No," reconsider your decision to keep it.

Keeping it cleaner

In *Plain and Simple,* Sue Bender describes her first experience of
an Amish kitchen this way: "We came into the large sunny
kitchen," she writes, "with its central table, black-metal wood-

burning stove, a linoleum floor and speckled beige Formica counters, something like the ones I had at home — nothing distinctive, neither old-fashioned nor modern. But," she says, "the room glowed. The feeling went beyond everyday cleanliness and order. The air felt alive, almost vibrating. Can a room have a heartbeat? Can space be serene and exciting at the same time? I'd never been in a room that felt like that."

What made the space so "serene and exciting"? Bender makes it clear, as she continues the story of her stay with the Amish family, that their home reflected their lives and themselves; it had nothing extra or inappropriate in it. It contained only what they needed and made use of. The surfaces were clean and clear, the organization sensible and neat.

Having made the first big overhaul of home storage to eliminate excess items and organize the rest, we're ready for the routines that will prevent us from ever having to face the big job again. When we learn to live clutter-free, to develop efficient cleaning methods and to work from an overall plan that keeps us on top of the maintenance jobs, both big and small, we will gain more of the time and space that characterizes a simpler home life. And we will be ready to give home a heartbeat.

Maintain a clutter-free space.

Clutter is anything that inappropriately takes up space on floors, countertops or furniture surfaces, and it is an enemy of the simpler home. It makes cleaning a chore and takes away from your home's atmosphere and appearance. Of all of life's problems, however, clutter is one of the most easily solved.

You do not clear clutter so you can reallocate the surfaces it once covered. You simply clear the clutter. The clean space — alive, glowing, simple — is the goal. In households that have developed the clutter habit, clutter bears a striking resemblance to dust. No matter how often you remove it, it seems to rematerialize within a day or two. Bad habits can be broken, but they need to be replaced with new, better habits. The De-Clutter Principle (pages 114–15) can help you to end the clutter habit once and for all.

A home without clutter expands, like a person's chest in the midst of a big breath of fresh air. It welcomes us to sit a spell and take a load off. It suggests new possibilities. It's simple and beautiful and completely within reach.

Make cleaning efficient.

With storage and clutter under control, the job of keeping home clean and life-enhancing becomes a far simpler one. We tend to exaggerate how hard and how time-consuming the task is. As a result, many of us fall into the trap of what Don Aslett, in *Is There*

Life After Housework?, calls *procrustination* — leaving things until they're crusty (at which point cleaning becomes the chore we've imagined it to be).

When it comes to the thankless jobs in life — those repetitive jobs that give results everyone expects but entail labor no one wants to do — you're best served by finding the quickest, most straightforward way to manage them. In the case of cleaning, a handful of commonsense tricks will make the job, if not painless, at least less laborious and much faster.

• *Equip yourself with a mobile cleaning unit.* Buy or refit a bucket for your cleaning supplies — a clean dust cloth, dusting wand and dust spray (for the cloth, not the furniture); spray bottles of premixed all-purpose cleaner, spot cleaner and window cleaner; fresh buffing rag and paper towels; and a trash bag. Carry this and your vacuum cleaner throughout the house as you clean. The number of steps you'll save will be more than worth the trouble.

> **TO CLEAN WITH LESS STRESS**
>
> **Maintain a clutter-free space.**
>
> **Make cleaning efficient.**
>
> **Develop a master plan.**

• *Equip yourself with good tools that are in good repair.* In one of the cash-strapped stages of my life, I vacuumed my whole apartment with the upholstery nozzle of a cheap vacuum because the floor attachment had broken. The situation was made worse by the all-but-absent horsepower in the vacuum's motor. In the amount of time I wasted trying to clean with an inadequate tool, I could have gotten a short-term part-time job that would have paid for a decent vacuum. Buy the best you can afford. It's worth it.

• *Duplicate specialized supplies and keep them in each room in which they will be used.* Don't lug around the special supplies for bath or kitchen cleaning. Those rooms need stronger cleaners to cut grease and to sanitize and should have a touch-up midweek.

• *Let your cleaners do the work.* Many of the cleaning solutions available today are designed to eliminate elbow grease. But we often undermine their power by rushing them. Read directions and *follow them*. To save the environment, try natural solvents and cleaning aids (baking soda, lemon juice and vinegar, for example). Your local library will probably have some helpful resources on the subject. Most natural food stores also carry books and sell natural products for the purpose.

• *Clean sooner rather than later.* Cleaning jobs become far more laborious when we "procrustinate." Dishes, windows, kitchen woodwork, vinyl floors, baths and showers can all be handled quickly and easily if you keep up with them. Let them go and you'll be stuck with those nasties — waxy buildup, grease, crud, scum, and allergy-aggravating molds, mildews and dust.

Develop a master plan.

Not all cleaning requires weekly attention. People with more room and less traffic may be able to clean some areas or rooms less often. They may find midweek touch-ups unnecessary in all but the busiest spots. They may prefer to hire someone twice a year to do windows and woodwork.

In fact, this aspect of the simpler life, no less than the rest, can be judged only by you. You know how clean your habitat needs to be to make you comfortable and happy. And you know how your home operates and what fits your priorities and preferences.

Spend time cataloging all the jobs needed to make your home clean and neat. Remember maintenance on furnaces, water heaters, appliances and finished surfaces — walls, floors and woodwork, decks, and so on. Separate the jobs by frequency. Be realistic, giving neither a higher nor a lower time rating than you believe the job deserves. Once you've got a list in writing, you'll find it much easier to plan how to keep up and to keep track of *whether* you actually have been keeping up.

With a master plan in hand, you free yourself from the time and energy it takes to be always inventing the next step. The overall business of cleaning, not just the weekly details, becomes one of the routines you need not reconsider more than once in a while (to make sure it's still working). You can easily negotiate who does what, because the whole apparatus can be viewed and discussed at a glance. And everyone comes out of the process with more time and less stress. Home ceases to be the place where all those chores are endlessly waiting for you to take care of them.

The De-Clutter Principle

What makes clutter so inimical to the simpler life?

- It creates an environment of chaos.
- It adds to cleaning time, because we have to either shift the mess, repeatedly put it away or clean around it. (Don Aslett, professional cleaner and efficiency expert, estimates that it directly causes 40 percent of all cleaning time and expense.)
- It adds to lost-and-found time. We can't have clutter without losing specific items in the general mess.
- It leads to late or nonpayment of misplaced bills and the resulting dunning notices and late fees.
- It adds to stress when company's coming.
- It multiplies our belongings, because we unnecessarily replace items that are lost in the piles.
- It causes arguments between those who make the clutter and those who wish it would go away. Just six simple practices can change the face of your home. Remember: Any activity you repeat daily for six weeks will automatically become a habit. It's true. Try it.

Habit 1: Put all clutter in its rightful place once a day.

How often do you leave the dishes, shoes, toys and books, and the day's dirty clothes for some "tomorrow" time to clean up? You may feel that you're too tired or busy to bother, but you need to take a second look at this habit. Find a time every night to put everything away. You'll wake up to a fresh beginning each morning that's satisfying and energizing.

Habit 2: Make trash daily.

Every time you clear the clutter, toss anything you won't use (junk mail, coupons, holey socks, daily paper, dry pen, too-tiny leftovers, dead plants, wilted flower arrangements). Create one small drawer space for "wait-and-see" items. Once a week, look again at the drawer's contents. Most of those items will soon become trash, and you may learn to recognize trash earlier.

Habit 3: Recycle constantly.

When the new issue of a newspaper or periodical arrives, immediately pop the last issue in the recycling bin. Don't hang on to old issues in the event that you'll finally get around to reading them. You won't.

Habit 4: Stop the clutter influx.

Write to the companies that send you unwelcome junk mail; catalogs; sweepstakes, credit card and club offers; and samples. Tell them to remove your name from their mailing list. Write "refused" on unsolicited packages (don't open them or this doesn't work) and return them to the mailbox. Borrow books and magazines, and rent or borrow videos (they go away).

Habit 5: Hold every capable member of the household responsible for their own clutter.

Daily. With penalties for noncompliance.

Habit 6: Use it or lose it.

Cancel any subscription that makes it to the recycling bin more than twice without being read. Date your pantry items and toss them after a year of nonuse. Give away clothing that you haven't worn in the last year. (You don't wear it for a reason; you just forget.) Pass along books that you know you won't read again. Assess anything that sits unused for six months.

Creating a harmonious habitat

Feng shui, the ancient Chinese technique for creating harmony and balance in our surroundings, is becoming increasingly popular in the West. A growing group of homeowners across the country are evaluating which way their doors open, how to place a single flower in a vase, whether the kitchen stove is appropriately located (on the south wall), and if they are allowing prosperity and energy to flow out of the house as quickly as it flows in. Perhaps *feng shui's* new popularity is one more indication that, in the midst of having plenty of plenty, we have discovered that our need is less for possessions and more for space and air, tranquillity and happiness. We have realized that the plenty we enjoy isn't providing what we want most.

The art of creating harmony in our living space — whether inside our home or around it — takes time and attention. Ideally, we balance utility with beauty, personality, rest and pleasure.

Don't expect to create a harmonious habitat in one fell swoop. Expect and enjoy a living *process* of shaping, tending and enhancing home that grows with you and your self-understanding, your relationships and your simplifying changes. Begin by shaping the smaller spaces within the overall space of your home and property, whether rooms, corners, passageways or gardens. Look at how to simplify and beautify the spaces you've created. If you make living plants a part of your spaces, focus on an enjoyable balance of

color, form and maintenance that suits your pocketbook, tastes,
time and energy.

Arrange humane spaces.

You can make any part of your home a calm and comfortable
corner. If some spot in your home affects you negatively —
because it's crowded, inelegant, dark, inconvenient
— that spot may be a good place to begin creating or
restoring the sense of harmony and balance that will
make home simpler. As always, start with reflection.
Remember that a home is a place for people, first and
foremost. Consider what changes will enhance
human comfort, sociability, efficiency and aesthetic
appeal. Don't let your existing belongings dictate how
you arrange your home, or you'll risk making a more
complicated, less humane place of it. Ask yourself:

*TO SHAPE YOUR
ENVIRONMENT*

Arrange humane spaces.

*Make small masterpieces
wherever you can.*

Garden simply.

- *What function do I want this space to serve? Is it a place
  for togetherness or aloneness? For getting work done,
  playing or resting? For guests or for family only?*
- *How can this space be simplified? What does not
  contribute to its primary function? What is missing that
  would enhance its use or appearance?*
- *How does this space reflect my personality, tastes and
  values, and those of the others in the house?*

Let the answers to these questions guide your plans for simplifying your home. If you put people considerations in first place, you may find that many of the material-centered choices will be far easier to make. Decorating guides can help you to arrange furniture to make the most of your space, but the particulars will be unique to you and your household. There is no one right way.

Make small masterpieces wherever you can.

Having made the human element of your environment primary, you still have to deal with selecting and/or placing the material elements — furnishings, decorations, plants, and belongings such as books, dishes, entertainment equipment and whatever else is peculiar to your life. A simpler way of living suggests several tenets that you may find it helpful to keep in mind as you shape your space.

• *Less is more.* If an element in a room has no clear function, experiment by removing it for a week. Rearrange the space as though that element were gone for good. When the week is over, decide what the missing piece added. Make a conscious choice as to whether to put it back or do without. If a piece of furniture has served mostly as a way to fill a space, consider a low-mounted picture, wall hanging or well-placed plant to take its place. Remember that less furniture, knickknacks and floor clutter make for more serenity, easier movement and less cleaning.

• *Color hides a multitude of shortfalls.* Before you decide that you have to replace old furnishings and decorative elements with new (usually expensive) items, consider some creative alternatives. Trends today include a broad range of refinishing ideas that can redeem aged belongings and give them new life. Use paint and cloth in a palette of colors that appeal to you to visually pull dissimilar items together. Lighten up the appearance of a dark or small space with mirrors and light hues. And use colors that re-create the environment you love best. Aqua, coral and touches of ecru may create a seaside feel. Warm green with splashes of peach, rose and yellow may suggest a country garden. Rich reds or blues, accented with gold or black, are sumptuous and elegant.

• *Personality is more interesting than perfection.* One of my favorite places to visit was the home of a dear former teacher and friend. Every nook of her home revealed something of who she was and what she loved. The pictures on her wall showed people and places she cared about. She had read and appreciated every one of her books. Her dishes were an odd assortment in blue and white and she could tell me where she'd gotten each piece and what she had been doing at the time. She left no corner unconsidered, as though she wanted her guests to find something to intrigue them whichever way they looked. I doubt that much of what she owned was worth a lot of money on an open market. But never have I been in a home that was more welcoming or fascinating than hers.

Let your home be an extension of yourself. Don't worry about the latest fashion. Fashion your home according to what matters to you, and let it speak your mind and heart.

Garden simply.

Whether you're growing houseplants, gardening in containers on a deck or patio, or cultivating a full-scale outdoor garden, keep a few rules of simplified gardening in mind.

• *Cultivate no more than you enjoy maintaining.* Start small. Add carefully. Stop expanding the minute it starts to feel like a burden.

• *Choose indigenous plantings.* Plants tend to grow best and with the least interference where they grow naturally. Choose for your climate, space and exposure. Move on to exotic plantings only if high maintenance gardening is your love.

• *Choose hardy breeds.* This applies to indoor as well as outdoor plants. The staff at your local garden center or a good gardening guide will tell you which plants succumb easily to pests, disease, drought or mildew, and which don't. It's worth the research to find and concentrate on the latter.

• *Focus on perennials.* They cost more initially, but they appear on their own after the first planting year. You'll have to thin, rearrange or replace them periodically. But you'll watch the garden come alive each growing season without undue expense or labor.

• *Choose low-maintenance methods.* The less gratifying work of gardening comes from lack of planning. Use weed block, mulch, intensive plantings and dense border plants to stop weeds and grass. If you're growing plants that need support, put cages, stakes and trellises around them early to do the work for you.

• *Plan garden spaces with people and function in mind.* Arrange plantings so that they enhance traffic flow, create natural privacy screens and add beauty to less attractive corners of home.

Gardens can add color, life and serenity to a home, but only if you have the time and money to keep them in good order. A thoughtful, realistic approach to gardening makes it possible for the brownest thumb to succeed at this aspect of a simpler life.

Home is where the heart is," Pliny said. I've heard others say that wherever their family is, that's home. In the Western world, we invest a large proportion of our home resources in material belongings. As we simplify what we store and what we own, and how we maintain and arrange our habitats, however, we may find that house pride and expensive, complicated homemaking slowly give way to a more humane view of home. Home can become a simpler place, where we have the time and peace to enjoy love and sharing, mutual support, rest, and harmony.

The Working Life

"It is too difficult to think nobly when one thinks only of earning a living," wrote

Jean-Jacques Rousseau. *And if Rousseau was correct, the inability to think nobly*

will certainly lead to the inability to live nobly. So we must ask the question: Do

we work to live or do we live to work? There's a difference. We need to know

which we want and then learn to live as though we mean it.

I love what I do. Marsha Sinetar, author of *Do What You Love, the Money Will Follow,* would say that that's because I "do what I love." According to Sinetar, discovering our "right livelihood" is the secret to happiness in life. (She wasn't the first to point this out. Buddha and others said the same thing.) It's also the key to making money, and we all ought to do it. End of chapter.

Let's suppose, however, that not all of us know what we love — besides family, friends, chocolate cherry chunk ice cream and the color of the Caribbean Sea. Or we lack the education, talent or opportunity to do professionally what we most love to do. (My mother loves to sing opera, but she'll never be invited to sing at the Met.) We may find our primary happiness in places other than work. Or we may not be in the position to leave a so-so job and pursue what we love in a tight job market.

On the other hand, we may already have a job that suits our skills and our sense of purpose, but we find ourselves in a rough patch at the moment. The size, responsibility or mechanics of the job may have gotten out of hand. Or our time is eaten up by the job. Or we're dealing with a coworker, boss or subordinate who makes a daily pocket of misery for us to climb into. We feel stuck and yet don't want to leave a job that has at its heart the makings of a happy fit.

Our unhappiness may come from our own basic inefficiency. We have been overtaken by piles of paper, backlogs in the in-basket and overfriendly coworkers at the coffee machine.

In other cases, we've been demoralized to see the prime tasks and greatest honors going to a cadre of up-and-coming younger people. Or we may have a career that puts us consistently in the line of fire. Do police officers, firefighters, prison guards or medical workers in the terminal wards enjoy their jobs? Should they? Some jobs are by definition seamy or unpleasant.

When we are unhappy in our work, for whatever reason, it complicates our lives and sometimes overwhelms us. It subverts our desire for a life that is simpler and more rewarding. We wake up with less than enthusiasm on Monday mornings and spend our days waiting for Friday evenings, our weeks and months waiting for holidays and vacations, our years waiting for retirement. Is this any way to earn a living?

In *Life Is a Contact Sport,* Ken Kragen draws a distinction between our "careers" and our lives. "The reality," says Kragen, "is that your career is simply one of the tools you use to lead a better life." As you consider ways to create a simpler, more satisfying life, how effective is your work as a tool in the process, and how much is it a satisfying part of that better life? The answer to these questions can guide the rethinking and, perhaps, re-creating of your work life.

Evaluating your working life

Remember that work began as the means to basic survival, before it became a "vocation," a "career path," or a ladder to climb for power, money and prestige. Though some of us live so close to the bone that we could not possibly survive with less, many of us don't. We may "need" to hold the job we have (or the two and a half jobs) to support the expenses we have built into our life. But the expenses developed out of that series of choices we've discussed before.

Carol "needs" the good car with four-wheel drive (the third in the family, after her spouse's and her college-age son's) so that she can safely drive 35 miles on the highway (at 22 miles to the gallon) to the job that requires expensive city parking and multiple classy outfits. Why does she need the job? It affords her the money to have the car, its fuel, her clothes and her parking spot. There's money left over for her son's tuition and books, but she could have earned that much money with fewer expenses in her hometown. There may be other good reasons why Carol chose the job and all it entails. But now she feels stuck and overburdened by the amount of money, time and trouble the requirements of the job demand.

Ken Blanchard, management wiseman, tells a story about a monk in medieval Italy who set off on a journey to discover why people work. The monk traveled to France and there happened upon a partially constructed cathedral. Numerous laborers and artisans bent their backs to their particular tasks all around the site of the unfinished edifice. The monk approached a man chiseling away at a huge piece of granite.

"What are you doing?" asked the monk.

"I'm chiseling this stone," the man replied.

"Why?" the monk asked.

"Why?" the man repeated, surprised at the monk's ignorance. "Because I'm a mason, of course."

The monk moved on to another worker, this one laboring at a fire.

"What are you doing?" the monk asked again.

The man gestured toward a rack where newly blown panes of glass rested. "I'm blowing glass," the man said.

"Why?" asked the monk.

"Because I'm a glassblower," the man replied.

The monk moved on until he found an old woman, slowly, steadily sweeping the smooth stones that had been laid to pave the cathedral's floor.

"What are you doing?" the monk asked the old woman.

"I'm keeping God's house in order," she answered and went on with her work. The monk did not need to ask her why she labored, for she had already told him. While the artisans saw their work in terms of tasks for which they had been apprenticed and trained, the old, unskilled woman saw her job in terms of the lofty cathedral that would eventually appear.

For many of us, work is a given, handed to us as part of our upbringing, understood as one of the essential elements to becoming a grownup. As young adults we may have had clear immediate reasons for working: financial independence from our parents, the wherewithal to marry or to start a family, the means to provide ourselves with material belongings or an education.

TO REASSESS YOUR WORK

Think in terms of activities.

Consider your personality.

Catalog your qualities.

We may also have had inspiring visions of where the work would take us. Nearly every child is asked, often many times over, "What do you want to be when you grow up?" The question taught us to think of our future selves as some category of worker. Taking into account our natural abilities and interests, as well as the responses, positive and negative, of family, peers and teachers, we set ourselves on the road to becoming. One job led to another. Added responsibilities and opportunities led to greater financial obligations. At the same time, any idealism about our chosen field may well have dimmed as we faced the humdrum realities of our job. Since then, many of us haven't had the luxury or, more accurately, taken the time to answer the question, "Why do I do this work?" We assume an answer we may never have articulated.

But remember that the central issue of the simplifying process is a vital connection to your own heart and a conscious

evaluation of all facets of your life. Integrity — wholeness —
requires a direct pipeline to your deepest values and goals.
Intentionality — living and choosing purposefully — draws its
power and life from those values and goals. Wherever you find
yourself now, if you want to simplify your work life, you need to ask
the question, "Why do I do this work?" It's not enough to say "I
chisel because I'm a mason." Like the woman in Blanchard's story,
you need to step behind the obvious and get to the heart of what
motivates you.

Think in terms of activities.

Your work may involve lifting heavy objects or it may happen
entirely inside your own brain. Regardless, you can describe what
you do in terms of action. Make a list of five verbs (action words)
that describe why you work. I might say, "I do my work to . . ."

1. *make something tangible*

2. *partake in a community*

3. *encourage others*

4. *earn a living*

5. *succeed*

Don't think too long or hard as you make the list. Just jot
down the first five verbs that occur to you. Then take more time to
reflect on what you've written. The list gives you a reflexive starting

place, but it will be most illuminating as you interpret it. In my list, for example, I discover that work means productivity to me. I hope to be connected and contribute to the quality of other people's lives. I also want to make the money that allows me financial freedom, and I want the esteem of others. Notice that I've associated *action* with *intention*. By moving the action out of the particulars of my present work, I give myself information about what *motivates* me.

Consider your personality.

There has been a popular backlash against identifying an individual with his or her job title or function. This has developed, I believe, because of the growing insecurity about employment that began with the breakup and deregulation of some of the big, "safe" companies (AT&T being a prime example). The loss of title and status that accompanied the layoffs and downsizings caused such anguish in the dispossessed that we of the psycho-savvy West began to recognize just how wrapped up in careers we had become. The loss of a job had come to equal the loss not only of a livelihood but of self-esteem, even of self.

Many of us continue to label ourselves according to the work we do, the work we would like to do or the work we believe we could do, if someone would just give us a chance. That's okay, as long as we remember that a person's importance in life is not defined by the job title he or she bears. There is a "human-being scale" that has to do with deeper meanings, character, values and joy. At the same time, who we are has a great deal to do with why we work and how we feel about our jobs.

Try listing five nouns (object words) that you feel could describe you in relation to work. Finish this sentence: "In an ideal work situation, I would be a(n) . . ." For example, I might create a list that reads this way:

1. *writer*

2. *teacher*

3. *organizer*

4. *athlete*

5. *connoisseur*

We have moved from an activity-based view of work to a being-based view. The words you chose should describe your fundamental makeup and your vision of what you *could* do, not necessarily what you're doing. In fact, I may compose music not because I'm a musician but because I'm a poet. I may cook because I'm a gardener. I may volunteer at the homeless shelter because I'm a mother. After you have found five nouns that ring true, jot down the ways in which you see these aspects of your makeup applied presently in your work life. Then highlight those items that seem absent from your present work. You have distinguished your sense of yourself from what you do. Activities don't define you, but who and what you are can generate the activities. And from that same source can flow other activities that might suit you better.

Catalog your qualities.

I once heard a wise man say to his complaining teenager, "There's no such thing as a boring day. There are only boring people." He was telling that adolescent that the quality of our life comes not from outside ourselves but from within. Consider the nouns you chose. What adjectives might you use to qualify those nouns? Fill in the blanks in this sentence: "I am a(n) [adjective] [noun]," and see if you begin to have a clearer picture of your working self.

1. *imaginative writer*
2. *optimistic teacher*
3. *persistent organizer*
4. *energetic athlete*
5. *exacting connoisseur*

Many of the adjectives that occur to you in one connection will hold true in other connections as well, especially as you bring your work life into closer harmony with who you are and make it a strong tool in the business of shaping a better, simpler life. An energetic athlete, for instance, has the potential to be energetic at any activity or pursuit that he or she enjoys and cares about.

Take time to study all three of your lists. If you feel that you've left out some important facets, expand your lists. If you decide that some of the items don't accurately describe you, modify or delete them. Let the words establish a concrete vision within you. You have intrinsic qualities for working — qualities in general, you might say — and that's what you've just touched on. That's what you want to carry with you into the simplifying process.

Making work simpler

How do we boil down the myriad, complicating aspects of work life so that we can begin to simplify? Of theories and voices there is no end. But among those many theories and voices, a number of common threads appear again and again. They focus on what you do, with and for whom, where, how, and to what end. These factors can act as a diagnostic tool by which to measure the present. They can also help you to frame an effective portrait of a potential, simpler future.

We could consider the six work factors at right as the pressure points of work life. Try rating your present work situation according to each item. If the item perfectly describes your work life, give it a 10. If it is completely absent from your present

---

TO SIMPLIFY YOUR WORK LIFE

Do what you love.

Work with people you respect.

Work in a comfortable, efficient space.

Do one task at a time.

Contribute to the lives of others.

Earn enough to provide for your needs.

experience at work, give it a 0. More likely, you'll find an item to be partly true for you. In that case, give it a rating on the 0 to 10 scale (8 = mostly, 2 = hardly, and so on). You've now begun the process of identifying the points of pain. Look at how you rated each factor in your work life. The lower your score, the higher the stress that factor is probably contributing to your life. It is at the points of greatest pain that you would do well to apply the most intense pressure toward simplicity.

Do what you love.

Some people hit the mark early and enjoy a lifetime of work that half the time feels like play. They're the ones who say, "I can't believe someone is paying me to do this! I'd pay *them* if I had to." Many more people either never considered that their love could also be their work, or they try without success to shape their love to the vision of others. When they later bog down in work that didn't come from the heart, they don't know what to do about it.

If you don't do what you love in your work life, you can make moves in that direction. Consider some strategies that may help you to re-create your work life in line with your passion.

• *Develop a mission vision.* Repeat the mission statement exercise in chapter 1 with your work life at the center of your reflection, building into your vision what you discovered in the word lists that describe you. The strongest first step toward a simpler, better work life is knowing where, who and what you want to be. Play with it. Write it out. Draw it. Brainstorm it, eliminating none of the ideas or visions that come to you until you've given your imagination full play. Remember: People often reach what they aim for. Aim for nothing, and you're *sure* to hit it.

• *Become a perpetual job hunter.* This is the best advice of human resource folks, headhunters, counselors and consultants alike. If you don't have a resumé, find a good guide to resumé writing in the library and create one. If you have a resumé, go back to it every few months to make sure it's up to date and as exciting as the person it represents. Look in the classifieds regularly to see what's offered. Even if you don't apply for some of these jobs, they may suggest ways that your present work could be modified or enhanced. Try formulating your own want ad that describes the job you'd love to do. Consider placing it in the professional journals or regional newspapers that are relevant.

• *Turn on your radar.* Be alert for opportunities. Almost without exception, the people who are now doing what they love report that they watched for any chance to follow their heart, readily said yes when the chances turned up and built on those opportunities to create new ones for themselves.

• *Pursue your love in your spare time.* If your current job is out of sync with or only tangentially related to your mission vision, but you don't presently see a way to change it, take advantage of leisure time to do what you love. Put aside the time wasters, eroders and bloaters (unplug that TV, for starters!) and give yourself the luxury of developing your love. Many people have been able to turn a loved hobby into a livelihood simply by continuing to work at it in their "off" time. If you need training or education, start getting it. Take one course a semester for long enough and you've got yourself a degree, which may be the stepping-stone to doing what you love.

Work with people you respect.

Everyone who has doings with other human beings has to deal with people they don't like or get along with sometimes. When these individuals are our bosses, subordinates or coworkers, it can rub at our souls, distract us from the work at hand and siphon off the pleasure of even the best of jobs.

Muriel Solomon has written a helpful reference book called *Working With Difficult People* that offers strategic advice on how to deal with a wide range of problem behaviors. In every case, she suggests that we first recognize precisely what upsets us in the treatment we're receiving; second, that we try to understand the perspective of the difficult person we're dealing with; and finally, that we step beyond the emotional reaction to a logical action.

If this sounds like a lot of trouble (after all, the *other* guy is the one with problems, so why am I doing all the work?), consider the alternative. As in all of life, we can choose to let difficulties ruin

A musician is true to himself

Even when he was a child, Evan's head was full of music. Tunes came to him as bright and dancing ideas that he picked out on his first guitar. As a young adult, Evan headed for California. There he struggled to write the music producers claimed they wanted. Gone were the lyrical tunes of his youth. When Evan met and married Kelly, he happily headed back east. He got the requisite "day job," but when their children arrived, the melodies of his childhood came back to him. He again wrote the kind of music he enjoyed, and soon his children and others were begging for more.

Evan became one of the parent volunteers who bring their talents into the school. He performed his music, and he taught the children to compose music themselves. The increased exposure of Evan's songs created a demand for a recording. Word spread. He has recently been asked to consider piloting a children's television program that would feature his music. Ironically, the folks asking are from Los Angeles, the city that used him up so long ago. In the meantime, Evan has held onto his day job. But he's having the time of his life.

our happiness, or we can apply the corrective energy needed to turn them around and make them work for us. In the long run, wallowing in unhappiness — acting like a victim — is a lot more trouble than taking constructive action.

The following fundamentals can help you to make troubled working relationships better and to build on strong ones.

• *Communicate.* Once again, we return to the "I" strands that weave a simpler life. A person who is self-aware and whole, and whose actions reflect an inner integrity, has the wherewithal to send clear, bridge-building messages to others. Never assume that people know how you feel, what you want or need, or the effect their behavior has on you. The more difficult a person's behavior, the more likely it is that they are wrapped up in their own troubles. Even the nicest person cannot be expected to read your mind.

• *Collaborate.* Pride, stubbornness and fear that we'll lose control can tempt us to work ourselves into a lone-wolf corner that makes our work less enjoyable. The skill of collaboration grows out of a sense of interdependence. If your work allows it, look for ways that you and coworkers can consolidate tasks, share projects and build on shared strengths. Richard J. Salem, a founding partner of a Florida law firm, became blind as a young adult. His sight impairment forces Salem to deal daily with depending on others in ways that we all should but often don't. "In my office," he said in an interview with *Self* magazine, "everybody's in the communication loop, and they're all encouraged early on to take risks, make decisions. The process may appear awkward or chaotic at first, but maybe what's happening is a different, more creative approach to a shared goal."

• *Delegate.* Are you responsible for work that you could hand along to someone else? If it's appropriate, learn to do it. Micromanaging or endlessly using up our time with jobs we don't want or need to do can become a habit that diverts us from the work we *want* to do. Choose one piece of work that someone else could do and assign it. You may be giving someone else the chance to develop their skills and move toward their own cherished dream. And you may be stimulated in your own work by their ideas.

• *Work for mutual gain.* When you're in working relationships, especially in a competitive environment, one of the most critical aspects to mutual respect and teamwork is what has been called the "win/win mentality." To build strong bridges between yourself and the people you work with, look for ways in which *everybody* comes out ahead.

1. *Always give credit where credit is due.*

2. *Search for strengths in others and give them room to use those strengths.*

3. *Treat gossip like the deadly, communicable disease it is; walk away from it, or practice turning conversations in less personal, more positive directions.*

A manager manages unwanted interruptions

Alice's office door faces a juncture of two heavily trafficked passageways. Because Alice is notably helpful and wise, people in her workplace had trouble passing her door without stopping in for a chat. Over time, this came to place an unwelcome burden on her time. She found her workload piling up and her patience straining, yet she did not want to close her door.

Finally, she hit on an effective, friendly solution. She had a friend in the graphic arts department make a cartoon poster for her door that pictured a caricature of Alice at her desk with an in-basket that was stacked to the ceiling. Under the illustration were these words: "I'm looking forward to talking to you — later. Let's make a date." Beside the poster she taped a weekly schedule that showed "talk times" daily, depending on the rest of her schedule. By setting aside no more than 45 minutes a day, broken into 15-minute segments that coworkers could "sign up" for, Alice was able to regain control of her workday.

If you're working with others, even the most individual of efforts has a larger, group product at the end of it. If every member of the team, from the CEO to the janitor, has a sense of shared mission, an in-the-trenches atmosphere can develop in which everyone wants each member of the group to do well and feel good. Team spirit can start with one cheerleader. Be a cheerleader.

• *Make appointments.* When you're interrupted, simply asking, "When can we talk about this?" will give you room to control the interruption. It's always fair to ask, "Is it urgent?" Then follow up with, "I'm in the middle of this report/letter/spreadsheet right now, but let's set a time to talk." You rarely have to appear unfriendly, but it doesn't hurt to look preoccupied.

• *Practice firm responses.* Requests for help, offers of new, different or more work, and demands that you do work that is not strictly your job are all part of the work world. If you know yourself and your goals, both short- and long-range, you probably know the appropriate response to any of these instinctively, but you may find it hard to give the honest answer. No one can answer for you. If you mean "No," say "No" and stick to it. Be professional, calm and courteous, but be firm as well. If, on the other hand, you want to say "Yes," say "Yes" firmly and do what you say you will do with energy and enthusiasm. You'll feel better about yourself, earn the respect of your fellow workers and make one more definitive step toward the life you want.

• *Ask instead of accuse.* Inevitably, problems arise that go beyond personalities and competition, that cross the line into the unethical, illegal or immoral. The cardinal rule: Assume nothing, no matter what your suspicions may be. If you become aware of a problem or are suffering personally because of one, *get the facts first.* If you can't uncover enough information to know for sure, wait and watch, or drop it. If after investigation you know for sure, then find out what recourse you have. (Check with a lawyer, the company's human resource people or a public advocate. Laws and company regulations exist that deal with many serious job-related problems.)

Work in a comfortable, efficient space.

The physical location and atmosphere of where we work may seem immaterial to some; for others it means the difference between a life full of complication and wear-and-tear, and one enhanced by surroundings that please and revivify. Start by making the most of where you are. But don't be afraid to evaluate whether a change of job or geographical location would make a life that is both simpler and more fulfilling.

• *Cultivate neatness.* What constitutes your workspace right now? Is it a locker? A corner office with a window? A drawing board in a cubbyhole space? Or a home office? No matter what it is, if it's yours, you can take the initiative to treat it as another room in your home. You may not be able to choose the furnishings, but you can practice the same principles of simplicity that apply to home space. Store only what you need. Keep backup material at the back of the file cabinet, or boxed and put elsewhere. Keep your supplies up to date and throw out broken, unneeded or inefficient items. Organize for efficiency. Keep items you reach for ten times a day close at hand. Put other items where you use them.

   • *Add yourself to your environment.* It doesn't take much to make a space personal. If you work in an office outside of your home, choose items you contribute to your workspace carefully.

   1. *Let personal touches reflect your values and aspirations, your joys, and your life goals.*
   2. *Consider ways to make utilitarian items personal.*
   3. *Carefully choose colors and materials that appeal to you.*
   4. *Include touches that add beauty and pleasing aromas.*
   5. *Have only one or two photos or mementos out at a time. You'll notice and appreciate them more, give yourself the boost that variety offers, and avoid the clutter syndrome.*

   • *Ask for improvements.* If you are not the one who equips your office, studio or workstation, be sure to let the appropriate person know about any faulty, uncomfortable or inefficient items in your space. The squeaky wheel metaphor is true. If your environment needs an oiling to be made more effective, squeak. You don't know what's possible until you ask.

Do one task at a time.

Psychologists and health experts identify one of the prime stress producers today as something they call "concept shifting." This refers to that nifty little trick we pull every time our attention wanders from what we are presently doing to some other thought, task, worry or hunger pang.

We have a task to complete, and we've already dawdled away an hour with sorting mail, emptying the pencil sharpener, clipping a torn nail and getting coffee. We're 15 minutes into the job when that missing letter crosses our mind. We drop what we're doing to start the search for the letter. Ten minutes later, we resume the first task, distracted and out of focus. We decide we need another cup of coffee but run into a coworker in the hall. Another half hour has passed before we return with the coffee (now cold) and a growing impatience with the original task.

According to the experts, we've not only wasted a lot of time and failed to get our primary work done, we've caused a lot of internal commotion. In contrast, researchers discovered some time ago that a person's chemistry changes in times of highly focused activity. The body releases endorphins, the happy hormones that give us a natural high and act as an internal pain suppressant. So, when we work on one thing with all our attention for a time, we not only increase efficiency and reduce stress (both high on the wish list of the simplifier), we make ourselves feel great.

• *Practice the art of mindfulness.* Mindfulness is all about being here and now. It's a quality that allows us to enjoy what we're doing and to do it to the best of our ability. Exercise mindfulness in simple ways in your "off" time. Then choose a work task to which to apply the mindfulness discipline you've been practicing.

• *Suit the work to your energy level.* Some work tasks are like cleaning the house. They have to be done over and over again, but they do not require peak energy and creativity. Consider these the "housekeeping" tasks. Other tasks are like building the house. They have the potential to carry you further along your path toward simplifying your work life. Consider these the "creative" tasks. Still other tasks supply the wherewithal to grow and learn so that you can do your work better or move closer to doing what you'd rather do. Consider these the "retooling" tasks. You can make the most of your work time by dedicating blocks of your high-energy, high-creativity time to the "creative" tasks. Use the "retooling" tasks as a productive change of pace when you've run out of steam on an important task and need a break. Save the "housekeeping" jobs for the slow spots in your body rhythm.

• *Work toward your bigger goals.* Knowing our goals and actually working toward them are two different things. Like New Year's resolutions, our best intentions often go astray, either because we haven't designed the short term in light of the long term, or because we haven't wrestled with the habits that have thus

Three Simple Focus Exercises

Many people have found that the following exercises greatly enhance mindfulness and thus their ability to focus on a single task. As their power of concentration increases, their efficiency greatly improves and their stress level is significantly reduced.

- *Perform a simple task and tell yourself exactly what you're doing as you do it.* "I'm picking up my coffee cup. I'm pushing back my chair with the back of my legs and standing up. I'm walking. I'm pushing open the men's room door. I'm walking. I'm turning the spigot. I'm rinsing my cup, rubbing the rim, shaking out the excess moisture. I'm looking at myself in the mirror. . . ."

- *Rediscover a familiar object.* Give your whole attention to that object for five minutes. Pick it up. Feel its weight, surface texture, temperature. Set it down. Look at it from every angle. If your attention wanders, set the errant thought aside with a "Not now" and return to the object.

- *Close your eyes and breathe.* Feel your breath in each part of your respiratory system, part by part. Listen to it enter and leave your body. Count the seconds for each inhalation and exhalation. Consciously slow your breathing. Imagine the air and its movement in and through you.

far kept us where we are. In *Nourishing Wisdom,* Marc David points out that it takes positive willpower to change a habit. "Many people are unable to accept their habits," David says, "and this lack of acceptance inhibits the transformation process." Start by recognizing and accepting old work habits. Then you can begin to work *for* your goals, rather than *against* old habits. "This," says David, "is the difference between positive and negative willpower."

• *Clear the decks.* Try emptying your workspace of anything that is not the work at hand. To do this as a habit, you may have to better organize your workspace and materials. Once you have a place for everything, you can build into your routine regular clearing. When you finish one task, put the materials away before you move on to the next. Make it the last task of your workday to leave your workspace tidy and welcoming for the next day.

• *Educate your coworkers.* To isolate blocks of focused time, we have to clear not only our workspace but our relational space. Other people will not know that we intend to work without interruption unless we let them in on the secret. Abe never answers his phone before 11:00 A.M., no matter what he's doing. He lets his voice mail pick up, and his message states clearly that he will return calls between 11:30 A.M. and 2:00 P.M. You may need to close a door, find an alternative (unreachable) workspace to do your creative and retooling work, or simply tell your coworkers, friends or family that you do not want to be disturbed.

Contribute to the lives of others.

When people believed that the world was flat, they would not venture far from home for fear of falling off the edge and dying. While we all experience real limitations, we are more often limited by our own small perspective. Our failure of vision or nerve to exceed our present experience is actually a failure of imagination. We become absorbed in our own concerns, fears and desires. The greatest satisfactions, however, invariably come not from what we *get* but from what we *give*. We make our work life simpler when we incorporate an attitude of contribution into it. We can't put it on. It has to blossom from the inside out, as we recognize our meaningful place in the human community.

• *Work from your heart.* No job is too small or insignificant to matter in the broader scope of our lives. Often we think that our work "takes" our time and our energy. In fact, as we bring more of our life into line with who we are, we proactively "give" our time and energy to work. Or we find a different job where we can. And we gain the potential to turn all of our work life into an act of love.

• *Do unto others.* We sometimes forget, even while doing the most meaningful work, that we have a personal effect on those around us. We get caught up in the mechanics of work and neglect the humanity of it. After I had major surgery, a young intern came in to remove my stitches. He barely spoke to me, hurried into the work and did not even acknowledge that I was crying out in pain until I grabbed his arm. What a different experience for us both if he had taken a moment to notice my fears and feelings. What do you most appreciate from others? A smile? Courtesy? Being given the benefit of the doubt? Being kept informed? Make your own top ten list. How many of your items do you practice toward others?

• *Practice right actions.* This is integrity on its feet. I find it fascinating that almost every image of falsehood or bad faith features a duality — a "forked tongue," "speaking out of both sides of your mouth," "double-crossing," "two-faced." These are images of division, the tangled web, complication at its most feverish. Do you want to simplify your work life (and your life as a whole)? Be, do and say who you really are and what you really believe. At least then, when life's troubles and conflicts arise, you can face them as an undivided person of integrity, with courage and confidence.

• *Envision a better world.* Feed your spirit with inspiring stories, visions of a greater goodness, affirmations of the positive values and qualities in yourself and others. As you build your dreams, let these be the mortar.

Earn enough to provide for your needs.

Before you decide what constitutes "earning enough," you have to *question assumptions about what you need.* This is a necessary, ongoing good habit shared by every financially independent person. And it is ultimately central to simplifying your work life.

The term *needs* is relative. A woman I know returned from years of relief work in Bangladesh to encourage new donations to the people suffering there from a prolonged, devastating drought. A group of service-minded individuals had gathered boxloads of toothpaste, books, gadgets and household items for Ruth. She described walking into the room where the donors had collected their goods. She appreciated the gifts, but she looked at them with puzzlement. She couldn't imagine what to do with them in a land where people had no food or potable water.

As we simplify, we come to realize the difference between *need* and *want*. The more we pare away the extraneous, short-lived and meaningless, the less we have to earn to support ourselves. As we decrease our income needs, we increase our work options (sometimes in direct proportion). Money ceases to be the primary driving factor, and we are freed to make work choices that give us more of the intangibles we long for — more time, less stress, greater self-determination, a better-rounded life.

Start small by keeping a record of work-related expenses. Include eating out, transportation, resources, supplies, tools, postage and shipping, space (if you're self-employed), and special clothing (any clothing that you would not buy for leisure). Once you've itemized the expenses, test each one for how much it adds to your "needs." Would a different, equally satisfying job be affordable without these job-specific expenses?

Think too about cutting home expenses (chapter 4) and handling your money more effectively (chapter 6). The more closely you look at all the financial needs built into your present life, the more you will discover the *choices* you've made, whether they relate to lifestyle, career goals or dreams for your family. Anything that carries a price tag needs to be rethought. You may be confirmed in your existing decisions, when all is said and done. On the other hand, you may find that your life has taken a few turns along the way that carried you away from what you truly value — while adding expenses.

Instead of looking for ways to grow into every raise or promotion, go back to your assumptions again and again. Today's money-centered society doesn't support us in this enterprise, so we daily face the challenge of making up our own mind about the human price we're willing to pay for the sake of the work we do.

Keeping work simple

In the movie *Dave,* the lead character, while impersonating the president of the United States, visits a factory. The workers there show him how to operate an enormous machine that functions as though it were a giant, economy-size pair of human arms. When

An insurance worker says "Thanks, but no thanks"

Mandy, a worker in the insurance business, found herself at odds with the pace and product of her job. When the company began downsizing and layoffs, Mandy was offered a substantial advancement and raise. The money tempted her, and the offer touched her pride. But she knew that the change of desk would not change the fact that she didn't like the business or her part in it.

Instead of taking the offer — which her boss went to great pains to say had been his doing as a reward for her faithful, good work — Mandy asked to be one of the layoffs. What she really wanted was to pursue a long-held dream of learning and practicing integrative acupressure, and with her severance package, she immediately got to work on it. The change made her lifestyle impractical and unnecessary, so she sold her expensive home, divested herself of most of her furniture, and rented a couple of rooms in the large, lovely home of friends. Does she miss all she gave up? "I don't want the 'good life' that you can only buy with money," she says now. "I'd rather love what I do."

Dave is hooked up to the apparatus, the machine arms exactly
mimic his own arm movements. When Dave boogies to the tune
of "Louie, Louie," the huge arms dance with him, and
the crowd of workers sing and clap along. It is an
exuberant moment that embodies a deeper theme —
that a job is not defined or fulfilled by its title or its
perks, but rather by the honest, goodwill outworking
of the human heart.

> ### TO KEEP THE SIMPLIFYING PROCESS GOING
>
> *Learn when to say "No."*
>
> *Feed your nonwork life.*

The simplest of jobs will complicate our lives if
it is out of tune with our spirit. The most demanding
will energize and enrich our existence if we love what we do and
believe in the larger, meaningful effort. No formula exists for
creating a work life that embodies what we love. We come to it
through awareness, small steps, and the creative use of *every* success
and failure.

Learn when to say "No."

One of work life's most treacherous shoals is the offer of
advancement. Many people take an entry level position on
their way to the job they "really" want. But what happens when
they have *that* job, and their boss or the company wants to move
them *beyond* it because they do the work they *love* so well?
Advancement almost always offers visions of more power, prestige
and money. These can be deeply enticing, but you can be sure that

they also carry a price tag. For many people, they require stepping away from hands-on involvement, carrying more responsibility, working longer hours, and dealing with high-stress and even high-risk conditions. You may find such changes invigorating and challenging, in which case the job may be "right" for you. But for others, such an offer may be the door to a blind alley that leaves them with more complication and a vanishing dream. Consider every offer carefully, whether it's a new position, a promotion, additional responsibilities or increased visibility. Test it ruthlessly against your larger, whole-life goals. Talk to the ones offering the job and insist on a full picture of what the job entails. Make a list of every ramification, and ask yourself: "Is it worth it?"

Feed your nonwork life.

I believe that many people sustain too-complicated work lives in order to fill a void in their life away from work. Perhaps their closest relationships are in disarray, and work provides a place where they receive positive feedback and a sense of worth. Maybe over time, they've given up past hobbies or failed to cultivate other interests, so that "off" time is filled only with chores or mind-numbing activities to decompress before sleep. Or they may have become so habituated to the adrenaline-pushed energy of a work-centered life that they feel somehow less than alive when they're away from it.

In any of these cases, the disease is an imbalanced life. The remedy is a conscious choice to refocus. If you're resonating to any of these descriptions, you will find your way to simpler living only by bravely facing the truth and deciding to work on the root cause.

If you want to avoid making work life your only life or a substitute for a fuller life, then concentrate on remembering the rest of who you are and planning ways to cultivate it. Whether it's exercise, cultural events, community involvement, social activities, artistic or craft expression, hobbies, or travel, find ways *every week* to nourish that activity or interest. It will take planning and determination, but the payback will be a richer, simpler life.

Most of today's trendwatchers believe that technology and the need to downsize are moving the world of work into a new era that will demand that every worker be an effective entrepreneur. This may sound scary and complex, but in fact it offers far greater scope for individuality in how and where we work, and in what we do. If we're simplifying in tune to our deepest values and hopes, the changing work world can become an exciting array of opportunities. And when our work, like Dave's machine arms, becomes a true reflection of ourselves, we may very well find a song on our lips and a dance in our souls.

Money Simplified

"I don't like money, actually," the great American boxer Joe Louis once said.

"But it quiets my nerves." And there's the rub. Just how much money does it take

to quiet our nerves? While we struggle to make a living — and to decide what "a

living" needs to be — how do we manage to make a life as well?

There's a saying that if it weren't for money, we could all be rich. Within that statement lies the central truth to simplifying our lives in a money-driven culture.

We live in a world in which money greases nearly every wheel. We find money handy to have and stressful to need. Many of us spend much of our waking life struggling to earn enough, if not to be rich, at least to live within some kind of comfort zone. What makes for "comfort" is an open question.

According to advertisers in every communication medium, comfort requires buying a wide array of goods. This will, they claim, lead us to love, security, prestige and happiness. (You didn't hear them say that on the ad? Just look at the images and listen *between* the lines.) To buy we need money. The idea of having sufficient money to accumulate goods soon becomes linked in our minds with the love, security and so on that we long for. In other words, if we want to be happy, we need to have and spend money.

So we put in our hours and collect our pay, do some wheeling and dealing, maybe buy a lottery ticket here and there, and grumble about the headaches of bills, taxes, inflation and the exorbitant salaries of athletes and corporate CEOs. We chronically have less than we want, and thanks to the miracle of plastic, we often find ourselves accumulating goods and services while falling increasingly into debt. We work longer hours, take on a second job, and yet the extra money seems to disappear before we can yell "Charge!" We want more. The question is, what is the "more" we really want?

Fortune magazine published an interview with Lee Iacocca, the czar of "more," several years after he retired from his superstar status as CEO of Chrysler Corporation. When asked about his retirement, "Are you smelling the roses now?" he replied, "I have too much going on. I'm bogged down in paper. . . . I want to simplify my life. That's almost a full-time job."

This man-who-has-everything sums up his experience this way: "You can plan everything in life," he says, "and then the roof caves in on you because you haven't done enough thinking about who you are and what you should do with the rest of your life."

Iacocca illustrates what Stephen Covey observes in *The Seven Habits of Highly Effective People.* "In more than 25 years of working with people in business, university, and marriage and family settings," he says, "I have come in contact with many individuals who have achieved an incredible degree of outward success, but have found themselves struggling with an inner hunger, a deep need for personal congruency and effectiveness and for healthy, growing relationships with other people."

It is easy in our culture to confuse that inner hunger for the intangibles in life with the need to have more money and what money can buy. The truth is, just as we have relationships with people, we have a relationship with money. The less we understand the nature of that relationship, the more complicated it becomes. When people step back and assess what they have added to their lives by driving in the "more" lane, their answers are revealing. Stress, pressure, a lack of "down" time, a load of debt and a shortage of satisfaction. Money does not buy everything; if we doubt that, we need only to look at the Iacoccas of the world.

In Your Money or Your Life, Joe Dominguez and Vicki Robin suggest that transforming our relationship with money happens on two levels. Money has value on a *tangible level* — that is, it allows us to meet our physical (and sometimes emotional) needs. But money also has value on a *representative level,* because it so often stands for love, status, power and freedom in our culture and in our lives.

On the tangible level, we choose how we want to live and our choices directly affect how much money we need. Choose filet mignon and a bottle of Dom Perignon, and you'll need a fatter paycheck than if you go for a burger and root beer. Acreage and square feet have a direct impact on the cost of living space. Two cars cost twice as much as one to buy, insure and keep in good repair. And so on. Name the items, compare the tickets.

On the representative level, we often operate on assumptions we've never examined or even identified. To simplify our relationship with money at this level, we have to return to the first "I" strand of simplicity — integrity. We have to assess our own perspective to unravel the areas in which money has come inappropriately to be linked to a deeper need in our lives.

Think of adolescent days, for example, when having the right label (or having no label) on your clothes became tangled up in your thinking with whether or not you were accepted (loved). The teenager may live in us still as we choose our style of living regardless of costs to win the approval and love of those around us. Consider the prestige of having a degree from a certain university. Such a degree may or may not show how bright or capable we are. It certainly does not indicate whether we have brains or character or a worthy contribution to make. Yet people who can't afford the Ivy League or its equivalent sometimes mortgage their future to acquire that document.

One of the many joys of simplifying is the opportunity it offers to question the givens of modern life. As we locate where we find our meaning and happiness, we gain the ability to turn off our culture's messages about money. We look anew at our real needs, both physical and psychological, and assess the actual "profits and losses" associated with money in our lives.

On the tangible level, simplifying can lead to retired debts, increased savings, the ability to live comfortably within or below our means, and the option of earning less in the first place. On the spiritual level, simplification can mean freedom from the money trap that holds so many of us hostage. It can release us from the myth that life's essential longings can be satisfied by accumulating material possessions. And it can give us the tools to shape our lifestyle according to our values.

Creating a money baseline

It's a fact of financial life that you can't reach simpler without first wading through some voluntary complication. You need to become intimately familiar with the details of your finances, and that takes some effort. When you want to renovate a house, you first have to know what it's made of, what holds it up, how sound the foundation is, whether its parts are in good condition. Without the preliminary work, any new work may bring the whole structure down, because you built on a faulty base.

You may already know your finances inside and out. If so, bravo! You're halfway to simpler. If, on the other hand, you're a member of the muddled majority, you've settled for a loose idea of how much you have, how much you earn, how much you spend and owe, and how much the government takes — the details escape you, and for reasons that you may or may not understand, you haven't done the background work that could fill in the blanks.

In a survey conducted by Drs. Ron and Mary Hulnick, psychologists and coauthors of *Financial Freedom in Eight Minutes a Day*, a full 30 percent of the several hundred surveyed admitted that they are afraid to take an honest look at their finances. Why? Fear of the unknown. They'd rather live in ignorant anxiety than know "how badly they were really doing." Psychologists call this attitude "denial," and we modern consumers are awash in it.

We fear as well that if we *know* what we have, we may have to control the drive for instant gratification that our culture encourages but that complicates our lives with debt and an overload of belongings. In this case, we're deceiving ourselves on two counts: first, that we can endlessly indulge our buying desires and never a pay a larger life price in stress and insolvency; second, that we can overspend our way to happiness.

**TO DEVELOP A
FINANCIAL PLAN**

Assess what you have.

Design a budget blueprint.

*Practice habits that serve
your purpose.*

Fortunately, there is a simpler way. It takes some effort, but it leads to financial peace and satisfaction. First, assess what you have. Next, use this assessment to build a budget that falls within your means. Then learn money habits that can allow you even to reduce your means.

Remember: While a budget can help you to learn how to pare down spending, it is meaningless unless it's based on an accurate picture of your finances. Faulty assumptions only dig you deeper into money complications. So start with the financial facts.

The cost of one man's ignorance

Wayne is a dairy worker who lives alone. Because his expenses are low, he settled for a guesstimate of how much he had from paycheck to paycheck. His savings were minimal, and he never reconciled his checkbook. "I let it go years ago," he says. "I thought I could never catch up." The net result was that Wayne made his occasional large purchases (a stereo system, a motorcycle, a computer) on a wing and a prayer. "I paid for overdraft protection," explains Wayne, "but it still felt pretty hairy."

Wayne's ignorance caught up with him when the bank made an error and shut down his accounts for apparent "lack of funds." Because he didn't know the bank was wrong and did not have adequate records, Wayne wasted time, and suffered inconveniences and sleepless nights, before he got his finances back in order.

He sat down with an advisor from his bank, who helped him to bring all of his accounting up to date. Once he had built that solid foundation of information, he was able to stay informed with a minimum of upkeep. In fact, Wayne has all the money he needs to live and to set some aside for the future. And now he knows it.

Assess what you have.

Begin by discovering exactly how much you have (your assets), how much you owe (your indebtedness), what money is coming in (income), and how much is going out and where it is going (expenses). There's no shortcut on this one. If you're serious about a simpler money life, you have to put yourself to this particular trouble, but the bonus is substantial.

• *Add up your assets.* We sometimes forget that our assets comprise more than the worth of our bank accounts or paycheck.

Imagine that you're about to join a group of interplanetary colonists who will permanently settle a new planet that has been prepared for Earth's overflow. *Nothing* you own on Earth can be used where you're going, because the new ecosystem and economy require unique materials, supplies and medium of exchange. To carry your assets with you to your new life, you must liquidate all that you own. That includes house, furnishings, decorations, tools, books, toys, music recordings, clothes, jewelry, cars, bicycles, investments, savings and checking balances, trust funds, insurance policies, possibly the worth of your own business, and any other transferable belongings. The sum total worth of these minus the cost of liquidation (taxes, commissions, fees) and depreciation (value lost through age and use) equals your assets.

Understanding the worth (and next, the liabilities) of what we own not only helps us to live at or below our actual means, it gives us a better sense of ways in which we might redirect our assets to better fit the way we want to live. For example, do I really want the storage and upkeep of Aunt Ruth's rare book collection, which I inherited years ago and have since looked at only when I dust and change the dehumidifying crystals in the closed case that holds it? What about selling it to a collector who will appreciate it and using the proceeds to pay down a 9 percent car loan?

Once you start the assessing process, beware of bogging down in the minutiae. You can take a shorthand approach that uses averages and estimates of worth. Just be careful not to overvalue the big items. With a little research, you can estimate fairly accurately the market value of your house, car and investments.

• *Determine your indebtedness.* The ubiquity of mortgages, easy loans, credit cards and "buy now–pay later" plans makes debt a major factor in modern life. We're so used to the idea of debt that we sometimes forget to take it into account when we're considering what sort of life we want and can afford. Yet we cannot know or plan from our actual financial standing without knowing exactly what we owe and the overall cost of maintaining the debt.

Indebtedness includes bank loans, loans on policies, car and student loans, mortgages and investment real estate, income taxes payable, accounts payable and payrolls, credit card and charge account balances, limited partnership debt, broker's margin loans, and other liabilities. The current balances on many of these debts arrive regularly in your mail as a statement or invoice. You can also create a document or spreadsheet for informal debts so that you include them in your reckoning and remember to pay them off.

When you subtract your *liabilities* from your *assets,* the resulting dollar amount equals your *net worth.*

• *Count income, past and future.* Most of us know, at least once a year, our regular income — from paychecks, dividends, interest, Social Security, gifts or whatever else — if for no other reason than having to report it and pay a percentage for our yearly taxes. We don't always keep the total firmly in mind, however, when we're in the process of spending it. Living simply requires an awareness of what money is coming in so that how we live reflects not only our financial reality but also the goals we have.

• *Calculate expenses, coming and going.* Our expenses — what we pay out — are probably the most mysterious of all our financial dealings. Regular fixed payments on mortgage or rent, property taxes, insurance and loan payments, tuition, utilities, and alimony or child support are the easy part. The flexible costs are trickier to track. These include food, home maintenance and improvement, furnishings, medical and dental care, clothing, transportation, child care, credit card payments, vacation and entertainment expenses, and income and Social Security taxes. When it comes to out-of-pocket spending, many of us don't even try to keep a record. Until we get a clear picture of how much we're spending, and on what, however, we cannot hope to understand our finances or to create a simpler financial life.

It's worth finding some simple way to record cash spending as we do it, even for just a week or two. Use a calendar book that

comes equipped with blank expense pages. Or carry a pocket-size spiral notebook, or even a single piece of scrap paper. Record each incidental expenditure. You need at least to keep track of how much cash you carry so you can add it into the expense accounting when it's gone.

Income minus expenses shows whether or not you're living (and spending) within your means. If expenses are consistently higher than income, you're falling behind. If expenses equal income, you're getting by. If expenses amount to less than your income, you can add regularly to the asset side of your financial profile. You have great flexibility to shape your future.

Design a budget blueprint.

Once you know what you're building on, draw up a plan that fits both your means and your priorities. Most financial planners advise the same three ingredients for a simpler relationship with money: pay off all debts, live beneath your means and routinely put money aside.

A budget or financial plan is only a blueprint. The plan is your guide to how much you can spend in a given span of time (weekly, monthly, yearly) and still stay within your means. Once you have the blueprint, you can go on to build the structure — that is, translate what you've created on paper into a way of living. Make the plan, prioritize your expenses and keep your plan up to date. This will allow you to make choices and develop habits that serve your pocketbook, your long-term goals and a simpler way of living.

• *Create the structure.* Don't make this a bigger deal than it has to be. You need only a list of your expense categories (you pinpointed these in your assessment). Make it as plain or as fancy as you want. Generate a computer spreadsheet or use a single piece of paper. In essence, you'll be creating one long addition problem, so list the categories in a way that will work for doing the math.

• *Fill in the dollar amounts.* Now the fun begins. Your job now is to fill in the numbers — how much you need in each category. Use the following five steps as your guide to prioritizing. Start with the items that do not change and must be paid. Then fill in the rest, leaving any "extra" spending for last.

1. *Start with fixed, obligatory expenses.*

2. *Use averaged estimates for necessary variable expenses.*

3. *Designate a set amount for debt reduction.*

4. *Pay yourself savings/investments.*

5. *Apportion what's left for discretionary expenditures.*

Prioritizing Your Budget

1. **Start with fixed, obligatory expenses.** Some items (mortgage, taxes, other loan payments) must be paid and don't change from one month to the next. Fill these in first.

2. **Use averaged estimates for necessary variable expenses.** Some items that we can't live without (food, clothing, fuel for home and auto) cost varying amounts from month to month. If you have good records, you can total what you spent in the previous year and divide by 12 for a monthly average. Remember that this is a number you will be able to reduce if you live more simply.

3. **Designate a set amount for debt reduction.** The best way to get out from under the burden of debt is twofold: resist new debts and make regular extra payments on the old. And the best way to ensure that you'll do this is to write it into your budget. If your mortgage payment is $1300 a month, pay $1500. If you can't pay off a credit card bill, pay as much over your minimum payment as you can every month.

4. **Pay yourself savings/investments.** Treat savings/investment money each month the way you treat payments that must be made. It's the key to a simpler financial life in the future.

5. **Apportion what's left for discretionary expenditures.** At this point, add up all the figures you've filled in on your budget. Subtract the total from your total monthly income. The difference is your discretionary money. If the total is already higher than your total income, look at all those items that are not in the first, "fixed" category and see how you can lower them.

Notice that third place in priority is given to reducing debt. It comes before putting money aside. And it precedes play money.

What's wrong with debt? In some cases, nothing. But the habit of debt — carrying a credit card balance, buying on time, borrowing for purchases or vacations — definitely complicates our financial life and wastes a lot of money. The habit of debt tempts us to spend money we don't have. It diminishes our future flexibility, because our resources are tied up in paying it off. In the long run, we pay thousands more than the actual cost of what we've acquired. I once heard a venerable senior partner in a small successful business say that owing money is like rusting from the inside out. You can look good on the outside, but your infrastructure tends to weaken over time, and you eventually develop unexpected holes.

Savings and investments follow quickly on the heels of reducing debt. Financial advisors stand united on this one. Some portion of every paycheck should be put into savings and long-term investments, no matter how small the amount.

Only after all obligations are met and good-health measures taken do you apportion money for discretionary spending. I like the "discretion" part of the word *discretionary* when considering this portion of a budget. According to the dictionary, *discretion* means, among other things, "the ability to make responsible decisions." A simpler life demands thoughtful, responsible decisions about the use of undesignated money.

Practice habits that serve your purpose.

Living simply is a lifelong process. This is no less true of the financial part of our existence. Two fundamental habits will allow you to continue the process of simplifying your finances to reach a simpler way of life in relation to money: maintaining good records and keeping your blueprint tuned up.

• *Maintain good records.* The only way to know what you're doing with money is to track it. Find a system that works for you.

Create a filing system that consolidates statements, reports and certificates that concern your assets and debts. Keep any original documents (some of which have monetary value in themselves) either in a fireproof, locked box or in a safe deposit box at your bank. Keep photocopies in your files. *Read and update the material* when you receive new statements or information.

Keep track of what you spend. If you love computers, invest in an electronic spreadsheet application. If you're a pen and paper advocate, shop at a local stationery or office supply store. Spreadsheets and ledgers abound, from bare-bones treatments to elaborate, pre-categorized varieties. Find the version that appeals to you and works for your needs. Simpler is usually best.

Keep a card in your wallet on which to record a week's worth of incidental expenditures. Save receipts and record the expenditures regularly. If you do it once a week, it will take no longer than 15 minutes. At the end of the month, you can compile four weekly summaries, again a small task. Make this record keeping a habit. It loses its "chore" status when done consistently.

• *Keep your blueprint tuned up.* Any kind of plan, including a budget, is a promise to yourself to follow it. After a period of tracking your use of money, you may find new, exciting ideas for trimming expenses, shaving more off your debts or streamlining the handling of finances. All of this can help you to maintain a money plan that gives you peace of mind and the ability to live simply.

To keep your blueprint up to date, take a little time to:

1. *Review your past year's finances.*
2. *Assess the choices you made. Identify the keepers; pinpoint any problems; earmark potential changes.*
3. *Consider what could be simplified in the year ahead and revise the plan.*

Finally, after becoming an expert on your own financial situation and creating a realistic plan for living within it, you have the tools to intelligently modify your financial habits and to enhance the simpler life you've chosen.

• *Simplify your upkeep.* A surprising number of people waste time, money and peace of mind on misplaced bills, overdue payments and pileups of paperwork. Others treat the whole enterprise as though it were a dreaded trip to the dentist. Half the journey to a simpler life is fueled by reshaped attitudes. Bills are a

Simpler Financial Upkeep

Once a day . . .

- Open and read all incoming bills. (Mail doesn't get easier when you put it off.) Make sure that they contain nothing (mistakes, mysterious charges, notices) that requires immediate action. If you spot a problem, place that bill in a "follow up right away" file. All others should be filed under "on receipt" or "by the 15th [or whatever date]." Use file folders, an accordion file or a designated spot in a drawer.
- Record daily transactions. It takes only a minute.

Once a week . . .

- Pay all bills "due upon receipt."
- Record maintenance, repair and unplanned expenditures.
- Follow up on billing questions. It may take a phone call or a quick note. Like other tedious jobs, it's easiest to just get it out of the way.

Once a month . . .

- Reconcile accounts.
- Pay monthly bills in full.
- Add up the month's expenses.
- Assess the month's activity against your budget blueprint.

Once a quarter . . .

- Track investments, pensions, Keoghs and other growing assets.

Once a year . . .

- Determine last year's net income.
- Add up last year's expenditures.
- Pay yearly assessments and taxes accordingly.

part of modern life. Give them some regular attention and they will lose their power to overwhelm. Follow the outline shown on the facing page to handle bills and money management. You can easily add or change any steps to fit your unique situation.

Some banks offer automatic payment services for certain fixed bills and payments. If you choose such an option, make sure that you review all statements carefully to verify that no mistakes have been made and to continue the good habit of knowing and understanding your own financial profile.

Learning to spend less

Becoming a pro at planning, allocating and tracking your finances will take you a long way toward a simpler relationship with money. But budget savvy will have its greatest impact when it's combined with less spending. Many people have found ways to cut costs without cutting what's best and most meaningful in life. In fact, they report that living creatively on less has actually enriched their lives both materially and spiritually. Having the means to live in a mansion and drive a Rolls Royce doesn't oblige you to do so, and neither guarantees greater happiness.

As you consider ways to spend less for a simpler life, look first at your *perspective.* Then rethink how you choose and acquire the *big items* — those high-ticket expenses that can leave you in debt and paying half again the cost in interest — as well as *food* and *clothing.* Finally, identify your own, unique *money leaks* and how you might begin to plug them.

Acquire a "less-is-more" perspective.

The habit of spending comes easily in our world. For most of us, the "victory garden," a seamstress mom, a Mr. Fixit dad, and children who play homemade games and do their share of the chores are long gone. Careers, school and after-school programs, packaged fun, and prepackaged goods have made it difficult to plan a life in which everything doesn't come with a price tag affixed. Try some reconditioning exercises that highlight the positive value of spending less.

• *Identify the difference between "want" and "need."* We've looked before at the power of language to shape our perceptions. This is true in our money life as well. Notice how often you say "I *need* . . ." Catch yourself every time that phrase occurs to you or comes out of your mouth. Then look at the object of the sentence. ("I *need* a new blazer [haircut, better car, good steak, insurance policy].) Could you honestly replace "need" with "want"? If so, that doesn't mean you can't or shouldn't buy the item. But if you get into the habit of recognizing the difference between necessities and optional purchases, you will see more clearly how to cut down. In fact, you may be able to take a second look at some of your basic budgeting assumptions — the "givens" you started with when you made your plan — and make changes you've never considered.

• *Think in terms of what you gain instead of what you lose.* It takes some discipline to break the spending habit. Chronic spenders often have to overcome a sense of deprivation when they pass up an item or event for the sake of living more simply. That sense of deprivation may have grown originally from a period of real lack, but it continues because of a current focus — generally on the immediate rather than the long-range picture. But what if every time we decided *not* to buy, we thought something like: "This is great! Because I'm not buying that . . ., I'm X dollars closer to paying off the mortgage. Once *that's* paid, I can work less and live my dream of traveling." What is your dream? Does the purchase take you nearer to it, or does it postpone what you most want?

> ### TO DECREASE SPENDING
> ---
> *Acquire a "less-is-more"*
> *perspective.*
> ---
> *Rethink the big items.*
> ---
> *Consider food and*
> *clothing options.*
> ---
> *Plug the money leaks.*

• *Choose what lasts over what is temporary.* Living for less doesn't require eliminating all the treats in life. It does demand a realistic assessment of what different options are worth. Asking "how long will it last?", "how does it fit my longer-term goals?" and "what could I gain if I don't spend this money in this way?" can help us to keep the bigger picture well in focus as we make the decision to spend or not.

I consider a gourmet meal at a chic restaurant a high treat. But it lasts for only two hours, and it costs. If I go with my mate, the sum subtracted from our discretionary fund doubles. Forgoing one such outing would allow us to buy a few new clothing items that could last several years. Ten such dinners could replace our old dinner table with a piece that would outlive us. Twenty of those meals could help us to build an investment portfolio that could make our later years comfortable and secure.

- *Replace the shopping hobby.* The "shop-till-I-drop" joke has its basis in many people's reality. Shopping malls and megastores that include all the amenities for a social gathering have made shopping a way to play instead of a restocking of necessities. The next time you decide to shop because you're bored, unhappy, looking for a social outlet or just "in a mood," stop in your tracks and think of five other outings or occupations you could choose instead.

- *Avoid impulse buys.* Marketing experts depend on impulse buying. They know better than we consumers sometimes do that if we took time to think about many of our purchases, we would be less likely (by far) to make them. Think back to the times you have bought on impulse. Where and when have they most often occurred? Is there a pattern that could help you understand why you buy impulsively? *The next time you see a nonessential item that strikes your fancy, go home without it.* If you still want it in a day or a week, go back to see if it still looks worth the money and other sacrifices to get it. If it is no longer there, consider it a gift of the thrift gods and get over it. *The next time you see something you know you need but haven't priced elsewhere, wait.* Once you've looked around, you'll know whether it's the one for you.

Rethink the big items.

Some aspects of modern life carry hefty price tags. Shelter ranks highest, followed by automobiles, depending on our choice of each. Major appliances and furnishings often take a sizable bite out of our resources, as do vacations and recreational activities such as golf and boating. All of these expenses figure prominently in the typical consumer's indebtedness, but they can also be offset or minimized. Just keep in mind that all your spending decisions represent trade-offs, then consciously choose what best fits your goals and desire for a simpler life.

• *Assess whether your present shelter serves you best.* For many, home ownership is a given. For others, it's a consideration or a dream. Some simplifiers have chosen to sell property and rent instead, because the monthly expenses are lower (sometimes), and renting frees them of time-consuming upkeep and offers more flexibility for relocating. Others prefer to own because their monthly payments (eventually) turn into equity. In other words, when they sell the property, they regain liquid assets. They also have greater control over their surroundings and a substantial tax break from the government. There is no one way to simplify the costs of shelter. As with the rest of simplifying, each individual or

A simple life lived richly

Maggie is a widow who has lived alone for many years, supported entirely by Social Security. Hers is literally a hand-to-mouth existence. To many, her life seems spartan. Yet she smiles easily, seems to cherish what she has and asks for nothing more.

Over the years, Maggie has maintained a simple saving habit. She takes all the change in her purse at the end of a day and drops it in an empty canning jar on her dresser. When the jar is full, Maggie takes the change to the bank and exchanges it for bills. Then she walks with the money to her community's center for battered women and donates it to their "Starting Over Fund." Why would someone who herself has so little give some of it away? "As long as I can help someone else in some way," she explains, "I feel rich."

household needs to assess unique preferences and requirements. As you assess, keep a few suggestions in mind.

1. *Find out exactly how much a year your living situation costs, including utilities, association fees, insurance, rent or mortgage payments, taxes, parking, down payments, and closing costs.*

2. *Consider a size no larger than you need. Remember that housing costs by the square foot. A larger space needs more furnishings, cleaning, upkeep and lights, and heating and/or cooling.*

3. *Pay attention to maintenance-related costs. Choices of siding, windows, and wall, floor and woodwork treatments directly affect whether or how often you need to redo them and at what costs in time and money. Insulation choices make a significant difference in utility costs. The extent and complexity of your landscaping has an ongoing price tag in money and labor.*

Never forget that your housing is a choice. You may be in a situation that isn't what you expected or that no longer suits you, especially in terms of a simpler life. Be adventurous in your simplifying dreams. It costs little or nothing to examine new possibilities. Changing the location, size or style of your home life can be part of a great stride toward the life you want.

• *Choose automobiles and major appliances carefully.* Housing can be an investment. With few exceptions, cars and appliances are not. They are expenses, pure and simple, and they should be treated as such. When you're considering how to avoid debt and to serve longer-range goals, you will want to weigh your options carefully on these purchases.

For instance, you may want to look for "new" used cars. People routinely replace business cars after 30,000 miles, and it's possible to pay as little as half-price for a used car in great condition that still has a couple hundred thousand miles of life left. For a second car that will be driven only locally, look for a used car without the expensive frills (automatic windows, cruise control, automatic climate control and so on). Some people find the "stripped-down" models more than adequate for all use, and there's less to break!

Watch for "moving" sales of appliances. Home purchasers sometimes want their own or new appliances and the sellers don't want the expense of moving their appliances to their next home or don't need them. You can find relatively new appliances in good condition for a low price plus the cost of picking them up.

When shopping for a new appliance, ask about upcoming sales. Also ask whether any floor models (considered "used" if they've been run in the showroom) are available. These too come with a price reduction.

• *Think in terms of using big items up.* A phenomenon called "planned obsolescence" explains the short life of some of the large commodities we buy. They're built to wear out within a limited number of years. You don't save anything by replacing items before they're used up except suspense — which can be meaningful if you have to take a car out on the highway, but need not be such a mystery if you pay attention. A couple of hints to carefree "full use":

1. *Keep up with maintenance. A machine lasts longer if it's kept in good repair. Read the owner's manual for timing.*

2. *Find a servicer who does not sell like items. He has nothing to gain by telling you it's time to replace.*

3. *Gauge the yearlong cost of upkeep against the amortized (averaged per year over the lifetime) cost of a new item before you jump into replacing, and keep your larger goals in mind.*

• *Buy no bigger or fancier than needed.* A simpler life depends on sensible choices that promote a saner financial picture. Think many times over about the relative value to you of an item that gives you more than you need. Extravagance often adds up to more than money lost. I think of a past neighbor of mine with a half-acre lot. He bought a slick, farm-size tractor to mow a yard that could be hand-mown in a half hour. Of course, he then needed a shed to house the machine, which used up precious space on a small lot and added a substantial cost. Was it honestly worth it? What would he have gained by sticking with only what he needed?

• *Plan ahead.* If you pay attention, you can anticipate approximately when a car or major appliance will need to be replaced. With some forethought and a little self-discipline, you'll avoid interest and finance costs by saving in advance of the purchase so you can pay in cash. Create a special fund earmarked for replacements and enjoy finding small sacrifices (forgoing the movie theater or an unusually expensive suit) that will augment a monthly budget line dedicated to it.

• *Question assumptions.* There's a machine on the market for every conceivable purpose. But just because these machines exist doesn't mean we need them. Always ask: Do I really need it? Is it worth the cost? What would I gain if I did without?

Consider food and clothing options.

We have to eat and we have to dress, but the related costs can vary widely. As with all simplifying, only you know the intrinsic value to you of your choices in food and clothing. Some people are perfectly happy with clothes from the consignment shop. Others consider a one-of-a-kind ensemble custom-made by a tailor part of the good life they want. Whatever your preferences, it's always possible to exercise money smarts in these arenas without compromising beauty or quality.

- *Organize your shopping.* Planning a week's menu and shopping only once a week almost always saves money, if for no other reason than that you save the cost of transportation and time. Make a list before you head to the store. Resist the temptation to buy items not on your list, unless they are truly oversights.

Do you know what clothing you have? If you've already simplified home life, you've gone through your closets and drawers and passed along or tossed any clothes you don't wear. Before you shop, identify the holes in your wardrobe and pay attention to colors you want to match for maximum use of new pieces.

- *Buy only what you'll use.* A tremendous amount of money is routinely thrown out in the garbage. We buy in more fresh food than we can consume in a week; or we buy items that we haven't planned a specific use for, and before we can get to them, they've turned into the proverbial science project. Imagine that you're a caterer. Count the meals and snacks you will eat in one week, and figure exactly the supplies for each. Buy only the amount needed for the time period for which you're shopping. Any more is almost certainly a waste of money.

Two tests apply to buying the clothes you need: first, "Do I have a specific, immediate use for this?"; second, "Do I love the way it looks on me?" Don't be gulled by how something looks on the mannequin, and don't let a friend or salesperson talk you into a purchase that you aren't certain of. As you dispose of clothing you're no longer wearing, consider why you haven't worn it, the circumstances in which you bought it and when you stopped wearing it. You'll find some clues to how and why you overbuy.

• *Use up what you have.* Try this food experiment sometime. Imagine that you cannot get to the store. Make as many pantry meals as you can conjure out of existing supplies. Commit yourself to emptying your refrigerator of all but condiments. You may be amazed at how many meals you're hoarding. In fact, you may be buying more out of habit than need. This is a great way, too, to revitalize your nonperishables. They shouldn't be stored indefinitely, so if you don't use them, they may join the excess perishables in the garbage — a needless waste of your resources.

Get to know your own tolerance for clothing wear. At the point that you no longer feel confident about a garment or shoes for dress or public wear, pass it along or demote it to "around the house" status. When it's too shabby for casual wear, toss it, cut it up for dusting, mopping or polishing rags, or give it "I can ruin this" status and use it for the truly mucky jobs — painting, pulling poison ivy, working with chemicals, changing the oil.

• *Be careful with coupons and specials.* You can save dollars on food expenses by using coupons on your regular items.

However, watch out for the coupon traps. Compare your savings from coupons to the amount of time it takes you to find and organize the coupons. Don't bother with coupons on items you wouldn't ordinarily buy. If you don't use the item, you waste its reduced cost rather than saving the amount of the coupon.

If nonperishable items that you regularly use go on sale, stock up. If you can use a quantity of perishable items on sale, go for it. Don't buy solely for the special.

Discount certificates and sales on clothing can be a bonus, but beware of the marketing ploy behind them. If you don't have a clothing need within the valid period of the certificate, or if you see nothing that you really want in the specific shop offering the discount, then spending simply to "take advantage of" the special has not saved you anything, it has cost you. And the store is banking on impulse buys once you come through the door.

• *Rethink eating out.* Remember that when you pay for the pleasure of a meal prepared by someone else in a setting other than home, you are also paying the cost of a restaurant's overhead, service and the enormous amount of waste a restaurant produces. You are also choosing to use your resources on a passing pleasure instead of downsizing your budget, purchasing something that lasts much longer or adding to your savings account. Eating out can provide a needed break or a shared experience that is well worth the cost. Just be sure to *count* the cost. Be conscious of the choice.

• *Keep the larger clothing picture in mind.* Many people choose bargain clothing stores and large chain stores with the expectation of saving money on clothes. For some the savings are real. For others, quality and style issues add hidden costs to bargain buys. Wherever you shop, keep a few points in mind for a pared-down approach to clothes.

1. *Buy well-made clothes in durable, washable fabrics.*
2. *Choose "classic" styles that survive the tides of fashion.*
3. *Limit your color palette. A few color-coordinated pieces can be combined to make multiple, unique ensembles.*

Plug the money leaks.

Replacing the washer on a dripping faucet can save gallons of water over time. In the same way, finding and plugging the leaks in our wallets will save us large sums over a lifetime. Value the care and feeding of the small change. It can become a satisfying habit in itself, and it offers a growing freedom from money concerns that will add incrementally to your simplifying efforts.

• *Count the cost of communication.* We add significantly to our costs when we fall into bad communication habits. For instance, if we wait until the last minute to ship or mail a letter, bill or package, we add substantially to the price tag by using overnight and priority services. Exercising the self-discipline to think and work ahead of schedule allows us to use cheaper mail services.

A homemaker tracks expenses

Gina long ago created her own way of controlling out-of-pocket spending. She took a set amount of cash from her bank account each week. When the cash was gone, she stopped spending for the week. Over time, though, she found that the money seemed to evaporate before she had bought her family's sundry necessities (including groceries and supplies). She was mystified.

Gina decided to track the spending for a week. She carried an envelope in her pocket at all times. She asked for a receipt for every purchase, no matter how tiny, and immediately stuck the receipt in the envelope. Or she quickly jotted down the item and cost on the outside of the envelope itself. At week's end, when once again she came up short, Gina sat down and created a quick itemized list by category from her envelope inventory. The resulting list gave her a very clear picture of where the money had gone. It took 15 minutes on Saturday morning and gave her valuable information on how to plug the weekly money leak. It was so helpful, in fact, that she has made it an ongoing habit.

Toll calls can add up in a hurry. Sometimes you have to communicate quickly, no matter what the cost. Most of the time, you can take advantage of significant savings by calling when lower rates are in effect. You can always cut costs as well by limiting the duration of a call. Find out what long-distance rates are and decide what you want to spend on this means of communicating. Time yourself according to cost and inform the person you're calling that you have only a limited amount of time. (Letting them know ahead of time can involve them in making the time count.)

Take advantage of special deals. Phone companies often offer a variety of plans that serve different needs and add up to real savings. Ask your phone company to send you information on the options available.

• *Notice the difference between leisure and luxury.* Special events and goodies have their place in life. But as in the rest of a simpler life, they need to flow out of conscious choices based on a recognition of the sacrifices they will require. Sometimes when we spend for pleasure, we're really in search of a sense of luxury more than some specific object. The next time you feel like "splurging," stop and think of alternative (free) luxuries: an afternoon reading, a long walk in a beautiful setting, a rousing game of tennis with a friend, an hour or two organizing your pile of family photos, a trip to a local exhibit. The best things in life really are free. They simply take eyes to see, imagination to conjure and a will to seek them out.

• *New is not necessarily better.* Many items can be found at tag or garage sales, consignment shops, estate sales, barter events, and secondhand stores that have far more character than new merchandise for a much lower price. When you have something specific in mind, take the time to look in the unexpected places rather than rushing to the department store. Remember, though, to keep your focus and resist, resist, resist those impulse buys that crop up along the way.

Step by step, it's possible to get our money life under control, not only in terms of what we have and what we spend, but also in how we keep track of our finances and avoid the money traps that are engulfing so many of us today.

Perhaps most important, we come to understand what money is and what it isn't. Money is not the deepest source of riches. Despite money, we can *all* be rich, and our lives are greatly enriched when money ceases to be a source of pain and anxiety. Obviously, some people have farther to go to reach "Start." That's okay. Don't despair. One small step at a time gets us there eventually. Only begin.

A Life Unplugged

As we struggle with the demands and complexities of modern life, we're tempted to

lay the greatest blame at technology's door. If it weren't for technology, we think,

life would be more peaceful, saner and simpler. Would it, though? Does

technology really make our lives more complicated? Or can we claim technology

as our ally in creating the simpler life we want?

Carl wakes up at 5:30 A.M. to the sound of his favorite "SeaSounds" CD, preprogrammed to start playing ten minutes before he needs to get out of bed, and linked to a full-spectrum lamp that simulates dawn. Meanwhile, the smell of coffee, set up the night before and started by a built-in electronic timer, fills the apartment as Carl signs on to the Internet to pick up his electronic mail. His first cup of coffee and morning E-mail accomplished, he hops on his NordicTrack (equipped with electronic gadgetry to record and display time, distance, and calories burned), periodically checking his heart rate on his watch, and flips on the TV for morning news and weather. As he exercises, Carl will occasionally talk into a mini tape recorder he keeps strapped to the track, to record thoughts that come to him as he exercises, or he will answer the portable phone he has within reach at all times. Track time finished, he pops a packaged breakfast casserole into the microwave, stretches, eats, showers and heads back to his home office.

"By nine, I've exercised, finished my correspondence, caught up with world and local news, and gotten a head start on the work of the day," Carl says, gesturing to the well-equipped office around him. With fax, phone and modem all on separate lines, he's ready to plug into what he calls his virtual office — the network of on-line business reps and distributors with whom he "interfaces" throughout the day.

When I ask him how he likes working without the daily face-to-face interaction of a real-space (or "meat-space," as some call it) office, he smiles broadly and says, "Sure beats rush hour twice a day! And I get about three times as much done as I used to when I was in a traditional office. I don't have to see the people who just waste your time anyway. Besides," he adds with an embarrassed laugh, "everything is so portable, I can work outside on my balcony on a nice day. Nobody even knows."

All around, Carl thinks the techno-revolution of the last 20 years is the greatest, and he is far from alone.

In contrast, some folks wonder. At the extreme of resistance are the "Neo-Luddites," a group of people who take their cue from the nineteenth-century Luddites, English weavers who, with their leader Ned Lud, destroyed the new textile machinery of their time that they feared would ruin their way of life forever. Neo-Luddites forgo the violence but agree with the sentiment. They want to unplug, return to the basics, get back to the earth and working with their hands, and deal with other people in real time and space — in short, to live "contraption-free," as Bill Henderson, a New York book editor and founder of the Lead Pencil Club, describes it.

Between on-line Carl and lead-pencil Bill lies a broad range of feeling about the remarkable technological advances that are daily transforming our lives. Whatever creates the perceived need for more technology, or the resistance to it, people in the industrialized world face a bewildering and often costly array of techno-gadgetry that is typically no sooner bought than obsolete.

What's at issue, and why is there such divided opinion on the relative value of today's techno-tools? Phrases such as "too much," "too fast," "too impersonal," "information overload" and "too intrusive" seem to arise when detractors talk about the impact of technology on their lives. At the same time, many of us enjoy the labor and time savings of dishwashers, word processors, automobiles and weed whackers; relish the conference call that allows not only business associates but family members in remote spots to communicate; and bless the day computer diagnostics became readily available not only in the world of medicine but in the automotive industry, in architecture and aviation design, and in weather forecasting and early warning systems as well.

In our more burdened moments, we act as though technology were an exploding volcano, an unasked-for act of God that we must somehow survive. We forget that its source is human. Our species has been busy inventing since we first decided we wanted a spear to hunt, a spade to dig and a bowl in which to fix our food. From the earliest wheels, pulleys and levers, we've moved on to printing presses, looms, oil lamps and electricity. Our inventions thrust us into the industrial revolution and gave us high-speed transportation and computers, and the ability to instantly communicate around the globe. All this creativity has poured out of the human spirit. Our physical beings could not contain or fulfill what we could think and imagine, so we created implements that would extend our reach.

Certainly technology in all its present sophistication raises significant moral, ethical and health issues. As with everything in human life, there is no one answer to the best or happiest use of technology. Day to day, differences in temperament, disposition, skills, interest, vocation and susceptibilities necessarily put us each in a unique spot. The decision about just how plugged into technology's gifts we need or want to be rests with each of us as individuals. Many of today's gadgets are so much a part of our lives that we no longer notice them or their effects. After all, the printing press, indoor plumbing and flush toilets are technological advances too.

A life that brings us into greater harmony with ourselves and our values does not depend on technology, but neither does it demand technology's elimination. The key to making technology a valued servant instead of a master or monster is identical to that for creating a simpler life in general. Insofar as we can, we consciously choose when, how and to what degree we include it in our lives.

As you consider a simpler way of life, take stock of the machines, tools, toys, chemicals, synthetics and inventions that are technology's tread marks on your life. Test the purpose of each in your current experience. Ask yourself:

- *How does this computer (cell phone, call-waiting, microwave oven, television, exercise machine, answering machine, fax machine, automobile, snowmobile, snowblower, lawn mower, VCR) serve my pursuit of what matters most to me?*
- *What does it cost me in time, dollars, distraction and learning curve? Is it worth the cost?*
- *Would I be just as happy without it?*
- *How might I consolidate its use?*
- *If I could start from scratch today, would I choose it again?*

Your use of technology need not be "all or nothing" to live more simply. You can take a subtler, gentler approach than the on/off options of the machine world.

Where do you start? The possibilities are as endless as the number of inventions, contraptions and advances that crop up every week. But once again, you can test for those areas in which you grind your teeth and feel your blood pressure rise. Then consider several typical areas in which technology can have profound effects: the *pace* of your life, the *noise* in your environment and the *immediacy* of your experience. Each of these factors will play an important role as you simplify your relationship to a high-tech world.

Slowing the pace

We find our individual pacemakers within. There may not be a particular organ we can point to, but we show our individuality in our waking and sleeping habits, speed of thought and movement, style of speech, preferences in recreation and travel, and ability or inclination to adhere to schedules and appointments. Technology has, in many ways, created artificial timing devices for our lives: we can rise and sleep without reference to natural light; we can use computerized tools that "think" and make word and image products at lightning speed; we can travel at such a pace that it takes days for our bodies to recover (we call it "jet lag"); and fast, efficient communication allows us to schedule our days down to the minute. To find that rhythm of living that brings out the best in us and leaves us energized, we may have to step away from our gadgets and let nature — ours, that is — speak.

TO RETURN TO
HUMAN SPEED

Hide the clocks.

Choose the "slow" method.

Let the phone ring.

Reclaim repair time.

Institute "off" times.

It is possible to choose a more humane pace in the midst of technology; in fact, technology can provide the means to do so. But you will first have to consciously own up to the ways in which you are daily driven by human inventions. Then you can look for ways that put you back in touch with your internal pacing. You can stroll off the fast track more often to enjoy the overlooks and way stations of life. And you can take the time to relish the *process* of life, rather than endlessly rushing toward the next *outcome*.

Hide the clocks.

When was the last time you spent a whole day (or even a morning) out of touch with timepieces? Plan a day off in which you cover up or put away every timepiece in your environment, whether you stay at home or head for some spot you've been longing to go. Make no definite plans, appointments or time frame for how you spend your time. Simply go with the flow. If possible, try doing this for a whole vacation. Then, while the memory of the day or vacation is still fresh, reflect on how you felt, what you did, how you did it and how the unstructured, de-clocked time differed from past experiences of "down time."

Choose the "slow" method.

Whether it's traveling, cooking, cleaning, making repairs, communicating, transacting business or playing a game, we've come to depend on technology to accomplish certain tasks quickly. In the sped-up process, we have sometimes lost the joy of what we're doing. Identify just one speed-oriented techno-enhancement in your life (cleaning, yard care, communicating, traveling). Try replacing it with the old, slow way for a week. You may discover that the "slow" way isn't all that much slower, when all is said and done. Or you may remember how grateful you are for the technology that has freed you from a time-consuming chore. In either case, it will be illuminating to experience the gains in human contact, exercise, quiet and thought time.

Let the phone ring.

At certain times of day or in the middle of an engaging activity, the phone can become a terrific nuisance. But it is our obsession with answering that traps us, not the ringing phone itself. There are other choices.

- *Hook up an answering machine and let associates know that you will check it at predictable times.*
- *Invest in a pager whose number you give only to your life partner, child's caregiver or emergency contact.*
- *Turn off the ringer when you aren't taking calls.*
- *Resist the trend to have a phone in every room. Try a good portable for the exceptions.*
- *Locate your phone away from eating and relaxing areas.*

Teach yourself to let the phone ring if a call comes at an intrusive time. Consider what it is that drives you to answer. (This will take some honest reflection. Phones become a habit.) Does it make you feel important to have lots of calls? Are you afraid you'll miss out on something interesting if you aren't available when the call comes? An answering machine may let you relax.

You can choose to cut loose. Important callers will call back. Casual callers will be discouraged from making the time-gobbling no-subject calls that you may find it difficult to shake loose from. The remaining callers can be happily missed.

Reclaim repair time.

Your tools and toys may be able to run without rest, maintenance or service for days, weeks or even months, but you can't. You need periods of time every day when you take in the nourishment that builds new tissue and fuels you with energy. You need physical activity to keep your heart, lungs and brain functioning efficiently and your muscles and bones strong and mobile. And you need times when stimulation and activity cease so that your body can rest and repair. Our use of technology — whether it's operating a machine or watching a movie — often confuses the signals our bodies send us. We forget that part of the reason we have the machine is so it can do what we aren't equipped to do. Because the machine is still running and there's still work (or play) to be done, we seem to think we have to keep working (or playing) no matter whether we're tired, restless or hungry. Remember how frail, ultimately, the human form is. Apply some basic health-giving discipline as you deal with technology.

- *Eat when you're hungry and drink when you're thirsty.* We often ignore these basic needs when we're plugged in. Don't! Let the machine motor idle while you refuel yours.

- *Move when you're restless.* People are suffering from a wide range of ailments that have to do with letting the machines do all the activity while we sit at the controls. You need to move! Stop the techno-action regularly and put your body in gear.

- *Go to bed when you're tired.* Television, the ability to travel through "sleet and snow and dark of night," and the World Wide Web, to name only a few, entice us away from the single most rejuvenating business of our lives. Wake up to the fact that poor sleeping habits are on the top-five list of killers, and get some sleep.

All this requires turning away from the machines and noticing your physical state, of course. Tie a string around your finger to remind you to do so conscientiously for one full day.

Institute "off" times.

When our region was brought entirely "off-line" by a storm a decade ago, the folks in our neighborhood banded together to share our defrosting food, take turns fetching bottled water from an emergency shelter, and share rides to the only grocery store in the area with a generator and a supply of basic goods. We came together in a rare moment of mutual aid and camaraderie. We also received a good reminder that we can survive a break from the most cherished inventions. Choose a machine. Pick a period of time and turn it off for the duration. You don't *need it*. You just think you do.

Looking for life's rest stops

Organizational experts Margaret J. Wheatley and Myron Kellner-Rogers (authors of *Leadership and the New Science*) have devoted their careers to considering the effect on humans of a world that increasingly pictures itself in mechanized, technologized terms. "Because we could not find ourselves in the machine world we had created," they write, "we experienced the world as foreign and fearsome. . . . But the world is not a machine. It is alive, filled with life and the history of life."

Technology tempts us to think that we can control nature and its processes. We "fight" the elements, we "battle" diseases, we "tame" the wilderness, we "conquer" space. While all of this has given us great advantages over our ancestors in longer life spans and ease of living, it has also encouraged the mentality of alienation and fear described by Wheatley and Kellner-Rogers. They conclude

A break from the breakthroughs

Kate lives in a rural/suburban area, where people live in single-family dwellings and have zoned protection from industry and overdevelopment.

"It's a good place to live," Kate says. "A good place to raise our two sons." Yet Kate's ideal is the Victorian cottage in which her family spends a week every summer. The house sits among a couple dozen others on a rocky island at the mouth of a harbor. The house has no electricity, phone or running water, and no vehicles are permitted on the island.

"You can't dash around, because there's no place to go," says Kate. "When the natural day ends, you have to find things to do in the dark or by oil lamp." She used to mind that the kerosene light doesn't allow her to read at night. "Now," she says, "we're in love with the night sky. We watch it for hours, and we're learning to recognize the constellations we can see. Just this year, the kids noticed that the water off the rocks is full of phosphorescence. We would never have known that if we had electric lights outside the house. Or if we'd been sitting inside using the Internet."

this: "As we change our images of the world, as we leave behind the machine, we welcome ourselves back. We recover a world that is supportive of human endeavor."

How do we "change our images of the world"? One refreshing, balance-enhancing way is to literally "leave behind the machine" for the natural world. Ways to do this abound, but for many of us, it takes a conscious act and a different quality of observation to genuinely reconnect with the living roots of life.

Have one nature adventure a week.

No matter where you live, nature is present. Look at the cracks and crevices of the most relentless city asphalt, and you'll see nature pushing its shoots up toward light and air. Critters find their ways into attics and storage rooms, chew through cables, and short out the power source for entire regions. Birds nest over porch lights, in scaffolding and on high-rise ledges. When we're focused on our invented efficiencies, we treat nature as a "problem." But when we touch ground to wriggle our toes in real soil and reestablish nature's balance in our lives, all those natural incursions become reminders, even lifelines.

Make a regular appointment with nature. Put yourself in nature's path and notice the wonder and mystery of it. Devote an

---

TO ENJOY THE
NATURAL WORLD

Have one nature
adventure a week.

Notice the scenery.

Eat a meal slowly.

Learn how to breathe.

hour or an afternoon or a day or a weekend to observing and participating in it.

- *Visit a park.*
- *Choose a country lane in lieu of a highway.*
- *Walk a beach or a mountain trail.*
- *Tour a nature preserve.*
- *Sit quietly for an entire hour under a tree.*
- *Walk a golf course after hours or in the off-season.*

Remember that technology can give you the means to spend time with nature. While you're at it, keep in mind that the most incredible human inventions can't compete with the tiniest balancing act of nature. It is your source. You are part of it.

Notice the scenery.

Don't fall into the trap of thinking that you have to make a project or an outing out of noticing nature's effects around you. The next time you make a routine drive, focus on your path and all the life you see along the way. If natural beauty doesn't figure in the scenery, notice people — their incredible variety, their idiosyncratic ways.

On one highway trip, I ran into the kind of traffic jam that usually happens in anxiety dreams. A serious accident had entirely closed the road and I was beyond the last opportunity to exit. I had no choice but to wait until the road was reopened. The wait went on for more than an hour. Because it was warm and all the motorists knew we were stuck, people began to get out of their cars. It was a strange event. All those machines, ordinarily barreling alongside each other at 65 miles an hour, had been immobilized, and out of their bowels came an indescribable mélange of humanity in all states of dress and mood and sociability. I've never looked at my fellow travelers on the highway in quite the old way since. They are no longer Toyotas and Buicks and Saabs that are in my way or driving too fast. They've regained their humanity.

Make a point of being where you are from moment to moment. Take in the details and enjoy them. Look past the machines to the faces that run them.

Eat a meal slowly, with pleasure.

Science has taught us to understand our food in terms of its component parts. Every packaged grocery item arrives by law with a breakdown of nutrients, calories and fat content on its label. Add to that the overweening concern in the industrialized world with weight loss, and you have a climate ripe for the advent of the "meal in a drink" or the "nutrition bar" or the upcoming pill that provides the "recommended daily allowance" of nutrients in a single swallow. These formulized, nutritional "systems" serve our high-speed lifestyles well. To fuel our bodies, we don't need to stop or slow down or use a fork and plate. We don't even have to exercise our taste buds. But consider the loss.

In *Nourishing Wisdom*, nutrition expert Marc Davis makes a strong argument for what he calls "conscious eating." "We don't just hunger for food alone," he says. "We hunger for the experience of it — the tasting, the chewing, the sensuousness, the enjoyment, the textures, the sounds and the satisfaction. If we continually miss these experiences, we will naturally want to eat again and again, but will remain unfulfilled."

You have the opportunity several times a day to slow down and enjoy a humane pace. Take advantage of it. Give 100 percent of your attention to your meal. Notice not only how it tastes but how it smells and looks. Feel its texture in your mouth and listen to the sound of it. Practice the old advice of chewing 20 times before you swallow and savor every bite.

Learn how to breathe.

If we don't breathe, we don't live. But unless we have some reason to pay attention to it — allergies, asthma or childbirth training, for instance — we give little attention to the fact that breathing is a moment by moment miracle of natural engineering. And within certain limits, we can control our breathing. Slow, deep, concentrated breathing can energize our minds, lower our blood pressure and calm our nervous system. Doctors, nutritionists, psychologists and physical therapists alike recommend the therapeutic value of just 10 or 15 minutes of controlled breathing a day. It's not surprising, then, that when we refer to slowing down and getting a grip on ourselves, we often use the expression "Take a deep breath." No matter what you're doing, you can always exercise the intensely personal prerogative to take that deep breath. Self-consciously slow your body processes as you focus solely on taking breath in through your nose until your lungs are full, holding onto the air for a count of three, and blowing the air out again through your mouth, slowly and evenly, until your lungs won't yield up another puff. Do this ten times in a row, thinking of nothing but the air moving through your respiratory system. Notice what it does to your pace.

Turning down the noise

Noise comes in many flavors. We recognize the roar and rev, clank and clatter of machines in operation, whether they're flying overhead, surrounding us on the highway or working on the office building across the street. We sometimes notice the din of the media — television, video, stereo, computers and information in all its many transmitted forms. We may forget that we are bombarded as well with ringing doorbells and telephones, buzzing timers and beeping digital watches, and humming refrigerators, furnaces, air conditioners, fans and electric clocks. The noise of modern life is so constant that we make unconscious adjustments that allow us to ignore much of it on a conscious level. But we still feel its effects, and we're left weary, stressed and sometimes sleepless in its wake.

A few years ago, I took a road trip into the foothills of the Rocky Mountains. It was late spring and the 8,000-foot-high mountain pass that I needed to cross had been open only for a week. The drive up one side of the mountain range was barren and treacherous, and by the time I reached the area of level ground at the highest spot, I needed to stop and compose myself. I climbed out of my car into a mountaintop meadow, still deep in snow. The sky was bluer than any I've seen, and the sense of space around me left me breathless. But nothing so captivated me as the utter lack of manufactured noise. As I stood on that high and lonely place, the only sounds I heard were the wind breathing past my ears and the beating of my own heart.

Since then, I've thought a lot about that moment spent, literally, above the noise of modern life. I'm grateful for the plane that flew me west to the mountains and the car I drove to the

TO INJECT QUIET INTO YOUR LIFE

Exercise the control switches.

Celebrate the sounds of silence.

heights, because they gave me access to a striking, almost magical reprieve. It wasn't simply that the wearing decibel level of a high-tech society was missing. I was given a break from what the noise signifies: "Hurry! You're late!" it cries. Or "You're in for it now — another traffic jam." Or "Look! How bad the world is becoming!" Or "Buy me" or "You're in danger" or "Take care of me!"

As you consider how simplifying your life might include a redesigned relationship to technology, take time to listen to the noise around you. Notice not only what generates the noise but what the noise signifies specifically to you. Reacquaint yourself with choices you can make to turn down the unwanted volume in your life. Explore what you gain when you purposefully "lose" the noise. Test the quality of time spent in an atmosphere of quiet. You will know how the noise around you has complicated your life only when you eliminate some of it and experience the difference.

Exercise the control switches.

I've heard people moan over the lack of time to spend with family and friends, read a book, head out on a bicycle tour, or take the class in woodworking or gardening. Yet they know every episode of *Seinfeld* by heart, they know the cast of their favorite soap opera better than their next-door neighbors, and they have a closetful of products they've ordered while "surfing the Net." In some cases, they don't see the correlation.

A simpler life takes nothing for granted. Notice how the media have been positioned in your daily experience. Pay particular attention to the messages you're receiving via telecommunications. Measure its contribution against your hopes and concerns, beliefs and intentions. Then make a conscious choice about its use.

• *"Break" your television.* No. You don't have to take a sledgehammer to the box or zap it with a power surge. The tube comes equipped with an on/off button and you come equipped with a finger to push it. If the television has become a constant background noise or an ongoing distraction (or battlefield) in your home, make a deal with all the household members to turn it off for a specified period of time. Plan ahead with alternative activities, and notice what you miss and why. Notice as well what you don't miss, and consider how to take advantage of television's benefits without being at the mercy of its annoyances. Pay attention to the ways in which your life is different or improved. Make "off" time the default position so that every "on" time requires an active decision.

• *Put the computer on a timer.* Advocates and detractors seem to arise in roughly equal numbers and a veritable war rages over the effects of computer technology, especially on the young. It may be a generation before we have a clear picture of what recent developments have "done" to us. But it's a certifiable fact that time on the computer is time away from everything else. Computers are marvelous, nearly miraculous tools. They also offer more than any one individual is likely to want, need or have time for, given a full and humane life. So it behooves us to pay attention to how we use this incredible tool and to manage its use and make it serve us in the best, most healthful way.

1. *Time yourself (or your children) to figure out exactly how long you spend with your electronic communication devices. Try cutting that time in half for a week.*

2. *If you have children, make a contract for computer time. Trade an hour on-screen for an hour of outdoor play or reading a book. Use a timer and follow up when the bell or beeper goes off.*

3. *Call a moratorium for a designated day a week. Expand it to two. Or three.*

4. *For each week on the Internet, take a week off. (It's like soap operas — not as much happens day to day as you think.)*

• *Choose the message without an ad attached.* Fine options exist in local Internet providers, live performances, advertising-free print media, public broadcasting, and recorded books and music that lessen the hidden noise of commercialization. A simpler life is often subverted by the commercial messages attached to our choice of entertainment, information and communication. We can choose the alternatives and free ourselves from what in the final analysis may amount to friendly-sounding harassment.

The death of a television

As a rule, the TV stayed on in James and Hannah's apartment from breakfast to bedtime, so when it broke, they and their two children felt the loss. They took the TV to the only repair person they could afford; he said he could fix it within a month. They couldn't afford a new TV; all they could do was wait.

With no TV to sidetrack attention, however, Hannah and James found that their two young daughters had quite a few opinions and stories to share. James discovered a knack for reading aloud. They borrowed music, games and jigsaw puzzles from the library for after school. Hannah checked out a book on furniture refinishing, and she and James began to experiment on several pieces they had inherited.

By the time the television was fixed, the family wasn't sure they wanted it. They reduced the number of hours that they watched, and when it broke a second time, they did not fix or replace it. Twelve years later, still TV-less, they occasionally see TV at a friend's house. "Either the programming is much worse," Hannah says, "or we were really numb back in the old days. There's just nothing we want to watch."

Celebrate the sounds of silence.

Marshall McLuhan, famed for his research on the effects of media, wrote of media's noise as a "counter-irritant." He suggested that we often turn on external noise to block out internal static — the discomfort we feel about ourselves and our own thought and feeling life.

A simpler life depends on mustering the courage to reckon with who we are and what it will take to move us in a direction we want to go. We don't discover this in the short pauses between blasts of external irritation. We find it in the still moments alone with ourselves, in the periods of reflection apart from the messages of others. We can slow our pace. We can also turn off the noise. And we can learn to revel in the grace note of quiet that ensues.

• *Find a daily quiet space.* Imagine a lake. On a blustery day, with all kinds of shoreline activity, the surface of the lake is roiled and choppy. The sources of disturbance are indiscernible because they are many, and the life that exists beneath the surface — fish, otters, frogs, reeds — is invisible through that agitated surface.

Now imagine the same lake at dawn on a still morning. The silent observer standing at its edge can see through the glassy surface right to the bottom, see all the life and energy awakening to a new day. Drop a single pebble on the undisturbed surface, and its effect is clearly seen as the ripples expand in concentric circles, bounce off the shore and come back as cross waves.

Just so in your quiet space. Without external noise and its resulting agitation you can come to see more clearly what lies below the surface of existence and of your own life. You can introduce a single thought, and in the stillness understand far better its meaning to you. Look for a quiet space, at home, at a local library, in a natural spot. Sink your teeth into the silence and chew it slowly, savoring every moment and letting it do its revealing work.

• *Listen to one thing at a time.* I recently walked into my home and found my husband on the second floor, running the vacuum and listening to music loud enough to outshout the vacuum. Downstairs was my son, watching television (turned up because of all the noise upstairs) with a handheld electronic game going simultaneously.

Multiple noise producers are often unavoidable, especially away from home. But think twice about introducing the din purposefully into your home or office. My husband says the music helps him keep his chin up while doing chores he doesn't enjoy. For myself, I've discovered (to my surprise) that the chores take less time and feel less onerous when I give them my absolute, undivided attention. (I exercise parental prerogatives with the video fiend.)

• *Institute an hour of complete silence once a week.* Many people in search of insight and deeper truths have taken themselves off to monasteries and other similar retreats, where silence and meditation reign for the duration. Ralph Waldo Emerson once wrote, "There are voices which we hear in solitude, but they grow faint and inaudible as we enter into the world." You need not find a retreat center to relieve yourself of noise. Silence is a kind of solitude that can be instituted anywhere. Whether you wait for a time and place that allows aloneness, or ask the people who share your living space to cooperate in a short hiatus from noise and conversation, you can make this a valued break to hear other, uncommon voices that can steer your search for a simpler reality.

Moving closer to "hands-on"

"Hands-on" is a relatively new expression. It entered the popular lexicon in the late '60s, about the time that a generation of young people were throwing out their razors, donning natural fibers, and experimenting with drugs and communal living. I've heard corporate executives refer to "hands-on" management, machine operators talk about "hands-on" training and museum docents plan "hands-on" exhibits. In all these cases, the primary point is the same. Someone is about to get involved with some facet of life in a close and messy way. The manager will deal directly — face to face — with the managed rather than working behind the scenes and through intermediate layers of authority. The trainee will actually lay mitts on the machine and learn in process instead of reading about the work in a textbook or watching someone else in action. The museum visitor will have a tactile, active experience instead of standing behind a velvet rope to view the exhibit from a sanitary distance.

I want to talk about "hands-on" living. In *Glass, Paper, Beans: Revelations on the Nature and Value of Ordinary Things*, Leah Hager Cohen tells the story of a Canadian logger named Brent Boyd who, in 1990, "became the first person in the Maritimes — the fourth in all of North America — to own a single-grip harvester." From the cab of his machine, as Cohen explains, Brent can travel through virgin forest, select and cut down a full-grown tree, trim off all its branches, and cut it into precisely measured logs. In many ways, the average suburban or urban citizen would say that Brent lives close to the earth. His occupation brings him into direct involvement with a major raw material of our daily lives. Yet, in fact, Brent is protected from the elements by the harvester's cab, cushioned from the noise by soundproof earphones, distanced from the hard labor by the machine's mechanical limbs, and able to produce the logs without ever personally laying a hand on a tree.

Brent Boyd's harvester bears a striking resemblance to what life can become in a mechanized, computerized world. Most of us have the potential to live our entire lives inside the "cab" of modern

> **TO MOVE FROM WATCHER TO ACTOR**
>
> *Plan what you've always wanted to do.*
>
> *Substitute an activity for one sedentary habit.*
>
> *Learn a new skill.*
>
> *Learn to appreciate each step of the process.*
>
> *Volunteer for one public service event.*

life, with machines and media insulating and isolating us from all the primary activities of survival. We need never grow a potato, butcher a chicken, nail two boards together, weave or sew a garment, or walk a mile. We need never physically travel to watch an event or communicate with a friend or deliver a package. Depending on where and how we live, we hardly have to step outside our door. And we don't need to make anything.

What we gain is the flexibility to choose how we will use our time, freed as we are from the physical business of providing food and shelter that used to define much of a human being's life. What we lose is immediacy.

Simpler living is by definition more immediate. Assess the level to which you have become a watcher in life instead of an actor. Technology doesn't necessarily make you a watcher, but it is important to consider how many *layers* of techno-assist, with its costs and aggravations, you've built into your work and play. Pay attention to the individual moments of your day and whether you are finding simple, immediate satisfaction in them. And begin to take steps to shape a life in which you can.

Plan what you've always wanted to do.

Most of us have dreams — something we've always wanted to accomplish, a place we've always wanted to see, an experience we've daydreamed about having. Identify one dream. Turn off the internal naysayer that immediately tells you why you haven't lived out and never could live out that dream. Instead, quietly, steadily begin to look into what it would actually take to make the dream a reality. Take a single step in the direction of fulfilling your dream. Try it on. Test it. Plan out what's needed. If you do nothing more than that, you will at least have left the armchair long enough to pick up the brochures.

Substitute an activity for one sedentary habit.

Physical rest is a necessary part of good health and vitality. Spending hours in front of a television or computer, sitting astride a rider mower, driving everywhere, watching other people playing tennis or volleyball or golf or swimming often pushes the envelope of physical rest and becomes unhealthy inactivity. Choose one habit that keeps you on your seat (one has already occurred to you — think no further). Find one active pursuit that can use the same time (one of those has probably occurred to you, too — one you think you don't have time to do). Take a long brisk walk, learn a stretching routine, take up a sport, join a gym, redo a room in your house, dig a bed for a garden.

Learn a new skill.

The age of technological expertise has not replaced handcrafts and foreign language studies, gourmet cooking techniques and furniture refinishing, carpentry, landscaping, hang gliding, tai chi or interior design. Nor is there any lack of techno-skills that can be useful and engaging to take on. Look around and find out what training is available in your area. Think about what appeals to you. Think about what would enhance your work skills, your home life or recreational activities. Check out the nonfiction section of your library or bookstore. Become the family photographer, the on-line geneaologist, the solar power expert or the therapeutic masseur. Embrace the learning curve that puts you in league with the doers of the world, but do it your own unique way.

Learn to appreciate each step of the process.

Inventive and engaged people love process. We of the modern world are used to instant solutions, whether they're occurring on a half-hour sitcom or promised on a bottle of ibuprofen. We're used to buying our food and other products ready-made and immediately usable. But nothing equals the pleasure and satisfaction of a job well and lovingly executed.

Consider a final product in your life that gives you great pleasure, a beautifully presented collection of photographs, for example. Take the time to consider each step involved in producing that collection: selection of just the right album; culling through piles of unsorted photographs to find the ones that offer the right

A dream realized

In her single days, Marti worked at a desk job for the airline. What she wanted was to fly, but the job description for flight attendants at the time left her out of the race. Twenty-five years later, with a husband well established in a career and their children grown, Marti noticed that an airline was hiring flight attendants. Requirements have changed in a quarter century, and ironically, in midlife Marti stood a better chance of qualifying for training than she had in her youth.

She did nothing hastily. She looked into what was involved. She conferred at length with her family, who would necessarily be affected by the lifestyle she would take on. And she took the first step. Step by step the pieces fell into place. She was accepted for training, and at the end of a rigorous period of schooling a couple thousand miles from home, she passed the tests that enabled her to fly. Is it all she dreamed it would be? She smiles. "I remember standing in airports," she says. "When the planes would take off, my heart would go with them. Now flying is my life's work. I absolutely love it and can't imagine doing anything else."

mix and have lasting quality; creating annotations that date and describe faces and events while also beautifying the collection; arranging the photos to best effect. When you recognize how each step contributes meaningfully to the final result you want, you learn to enjoy the separate pieces of the process.

Volunteer for one public service event.

A feeling of helplessness in the face of politics and public life is endemic in modern society. Problems of pollution, ozone depletion, invadable computer data banks and a shaky global economy tempt us to hide our heads. But around the world grassroots efforts have changed the landscape. Many communities have instituted as simple an effort as regular "cleanup" days for parks, roadways or beaches. Families, kids' clubs and community groups have made a lasting impact on the beauty of their surroundings and had fun at the same time!

Before you resign yourself to watching world events in fear and disgruntlement, consider turning off the TV news, laying aside the latest alarmist reports, and instead finding out what local groups are active in your community. Efforts such as Habitat for Humanity have taken a hand in addressing some of the basic needs of the poor. Others have gotten involved in bringing cheer to shut-ins or the terminally ill. These efforts are run on the goodwill and volunteerism of ordinary people who have chosen to get involved.

Not a day goes by that the news doesn't announce another scientific advance, a new computer, a successful cloning, artificial body parts, artificial intelligence or new breakthroughs in virtual experiences of one sort or another. It isn't likely to end or even to slow down.

Neither is it the end of the world. We are still human; we still give birth, fall in love, start revolutions and die of natural causes. We have the ability to choose what we do with the flowering of technology. And many people are making intelligent, active choices. Thus the popularity of "living wills" that enable people to indicate ahead of time their desires, should their lives at some point depend entirely on artificial life support. Thus the resurgence of natural childbirth that takes advantage of medicine's critical intervention only when needed. Thus the interest in alternative medicine, organic farming, wilderness training and the protection of watershed areas.

We can choose how and when to embrace the world of technology and virtual advances and still keep our feet firmly planted in real time and space. Look for the many opportunities that surround you every day to enjoy "actual" reality. It's hands-on, and that means you sometimes get your hands dirty. Go ahead. Get a little grubby. It's life!

Simply Continuing

Life is a gift, waiting every day to be unwrapped anew. We choose to be conscious

of the gift when we choose a simpler life. We take responsibility for the gift,

understanding that it is ours to use or waste. Every day.

Some people dream of a simpler life. Some people do more than dream. They make it their reality. The difference between the dreamers and the doers is their willingness to take a chance. Simplifying is risky. We have to give up the status quo. We have to take a clear-eyed look at our lives, to question past decisions and assumptions and be ready to make changes — small and large. Sometimes, we have to venture into entirely new territory. The simpler life doesn't come prepackaged. It is custom-made, person by person. We are each of us so remarkably one-of-a-kind that only a one-of-a-kind combination of choices and actions will add up to a simpler way. But if we're adventurous enough, we don't have to settle for dreaming. We can live the dream.

Why do we take the chance? What does the simpler life offer that makes the risk worth taking?

First and foremost is *freedom*. If I had it in my power to offer only one gift to others, it would be the gift of freedom. But freedom is a gift that can't be handed, ready-made and instantly usable, to others. Freedom has to be recognized and exercised from the inside out. When we decide to live more simply, we exercise the freedom to be ourselves and to choose the way we want to live.

The simpler life gives us *time*. An enormous amount of scientific research is dedicated to finding ways to increase our time on this earth. Fashioning a simpler life for ourselves takes time. But that new life also gives time back to us, multiplied. We may not live a day longer than we would have otherwise (although maybe we will). We will certainly gain a greater measure of timeless time — the essence of moments well and *fully* lived — and more of our days will consist of that high-quality time.

As we simplify, we also gain *flexibility*. Picture a giant, ancient tree that has weathered hurricanes and ice storms, drought and gloom. Central to the tree's success is its ability to bend and sway, to send roots deeper and branches higher — in other words, to adapt for its own best existence. A simpler perspective opens the possibility of bend and sway, depth and reach in our lives. When we discover how we can live *with* less and *for* less, we find that many more options exist for us to make life adjustments that lead to happiness. We broaden our choices about where and how we will live, how much we'll work and at what, and how we will relate to those around us.

And the simpler life offers us *rest*. I'm not talking about physical rest only, although that's part of it. I'm talking about rest for our spirits. At times in my life, I have felt that I would have traded everything I owned for a sense of peace. I didn't realize then that the pathway to my soul's rest could actually have something to do with trading some of what I owned — not just belongings but attitudes, habits, fears and expectations — for a better way.

The gifts of a simpler life begin to appear as soon as we start to translate the dream of simplicity into specific choices and actions. The gifts grow over time. Simplicity is, at heart, living in concert with ourselves. The longer we make simplicity a way of life, the better we become at living true to ourselves, and the greater our experience is of freedom and flexibility, high-quality time and soul-deep rest. Our life fits us better and we enjoy it more and more.

But life is not a coat. We can't tailor it once and for all to make the perfect fit. We keep changing. Our circumstances develop, shift, fall apart and come together again in a new shape. These are not the harsh truths of life. They are the wonder of it.

So how do we make simplifying more than a passing phase in our life, more than some fad diet or exercise program that works for a while but eventually is left behind?

We can start by not being so surprised and offended every time life throws us a curve. We aren't being singled out for special treatment when our simpler life is challenged. Complications are always on the doorstep, waiting for a chance to come in. Not just for me or you. For everyone. Inevitably, some will arrive uninvited — an unexpected baby, the loss of a loved one, a downturn in our work life, an illness. Others we may initiate — a new opportunity, a new relationship, a change of location. Either way, they are a part of everyone's existence, and the sooner we accept that, the better able we'll be to keep our lives as simple as we want.

We can also recognize that simplicity is more than the sum of what's left after we've eliminated complications from our lives. It is a way of thinking and seeing, a state of being, a response, and a commitment. When we stop thinking of the simpler life as something outside of ourselves, we take a significant step toward making simplicity a path that lasts a lifetime. The simpler life has begun. Now we move ahead.

Keeping life simpler

"I believe we would be happier to have a personal revolution in our individual lives and go back to simpler living and more direct thinking," American author Laura Ingalls Wilder once wrote. "It is the simple things of life that make living worthwhile, the sweet fundamental things such as love and duty, work and rest and living close to nature."

I especially appreciate Wilder's image of a "personal revolution." It conjures up a mood of radical involvement. If we want the "sweet fundamental things of life" to thrive in our simpler life, we need to *keep* choosing them. It's an ongoing overhaul that we actively support. The process resembles what we did to *start* a simpler life, only now we already have the foundation in place to build the life we want. And we're becoming more familiar with the tools we will use for a lifetime.

Keeping life simpler requires an attitude of assessment. We consciously take account of where we are and where we're headed. We appreciate the space we've cleared around and in us and make it work for us. We face what comes our way with grace and purpose. And we continue to change and develop in line with who we are and the direction we've chosen. The simpler life is a fully conscious life, a life worth living.

Keep assessing.

We begin the simplifying process with a conscious assessment of who we are, what matters to us, and where we stand in relation to time, other people, our home and work lives, our personal resources, and our era in human history. We continue the process by making that conscious assessment a way of life.

It's tempting to think that as long as we're not sleeping or in a coma, we're living consciously. But in our honest moments, most of us will admit that we don't always want to put ourselves to the trouble of asking the hard questions or swimming against the current. Unfortunately, the alternative is letting our lives be molded for us instead of making an original work of them. A life lived in less than a fully conscious state will revert to a complicated one, because we stop recognizing the *alternative* choices available to us. Before we know it, we are once again living out of sync with ourselves and what matters most to us.

Keep up the good work of turning aspects of your life over and looking at them from different angles. When you find yourself frazzled or burdened or out-of-sorts for more than a single "off" day, don't ignore it. And don't let yourself fall back on old thought habits that settle for the status quo or inactive complaining. Examine what *seems* to be the problem (the "presenting" problem, as a counselor might say). Then look behind it and underneath it until you uncover what has really moved you off balance in your simpler life. Face what's out of whack and do something about it.

> ### TO CONTINUE THE SIMPLER LIFE
>
> *Keep assessing.*
>
> *Pursue what's missing.*
>
> *Face new complications as challenges.*
>
> *Carry simplicity within you.*

Pursue what's missing.

When we work to simplify our lives, we generally aim to have less stuff around us or fewer complications to deal with. Part of simplifying is consciously unloading the excess in our lives — pulling the weeds — that we accumulate. You can be sure, however, that if you make an empty space without cultivating it, it will quickly fill up again, with new or returned complications and misfits. As we continue to assess, we discover that nature really does abhor a vacuum. Pull one weed out of the garden and another will inevitably grow in its place. Cultivation is the conscious appreciation and use of the ground we clear. And it requires a plan, a sense of purpose, a deliberate act.

As you think about your simplified life, move your thoughts from what you've eliminated to what you might gain or have already gained. It may be rest, pure and simple. But it can be much more. Ask yourself: Where does my heart incline? What deeper hungers surface in my quiet moments? With these questions in mind, turn the cultivation of your simpler life into a treasure hunt.

Follow the hunt, like a hound following a scent. This is one way that you put those gifts of simplicity — freedom, flexibility, time and rest — to good use. In the process, you can *enlarge* rather than complicate your life. You can replace old frustrations with fulfilled dreams.

This is sometimes easier said than done, of course. The more we simplify, the more new territory we discover. We may not be prepared to find the riches awaiting us. To make the most of our simpler life, we need to keep sharpening our senses. Consider the ways in which you can hone your response to possibilities. Ask:

- *What am I doing to nourish my spirit so that I have the moral and ethical stamina to make a better life?*

- *In what ways am I pushing out my personal boundaries, questioning my assumptions about what life offers and how I fit into it?*

- *What do I hope for? What do I want to stand for and accomplish, both in the near future and over the course of my life? How does my life reflect this?*

A teacher keeps teaching simpler

Deb originally took a position as a French teacher in an alternative school because, with small classes, it allowed her to teach in the way she wanted. She could develop new programs, try new methods and create more innovative challenges for her students.

Over time, however, the school grew, and so did class sizes. Within a few years, Deb found that she quickly bogged down each fall under the weight of too many, too-large classes.

Deb wanted the time and freedom to continue doing her job with excellence. Because the school paid teachers according to their workload, Deb knew that she might be able to arrange a better teaching schedule for herself if she were willing to free up resources (part of her salary) for an additional teacher.

Deb assessed her expenses and saw that many luxuries had crept into her simple lifestyle. Choosing to earn less would mean making changes. The choice was easy. Doing her job well meant far more to her than the luxuries she would forgo. It was a choice in favor of continuing a simpler life that was rich in meaning.

Ask these questions regularly. The answers are unique to you, but they will yield up the treasure map that leads to the best of what a simpler life offers.

Face new complications as challenges.

It would be great to simplify, make the most of the simpler life we've created and then sit back with a satisfied "A-a-ah," never to be troubled by life's complications again. A once-and-for-all fix. But anyone who has spent some time on this planet knows that it doesn't work that way, at least not for long. Life has a way of complicating itself time and again. In the context of a simpler life, however, complications don't have to be our undoing.

Some complications in life are difficulties. Some are exciting, enticing new possibilities. In either case, we can choose our response. In fact, once we simplify, we have more emotional, material and physical resources available to us to make that choice. In bygone days, we may have developed a habitual response of feeling overwhelmed at every new complication. The response was appropriate because we were dealing with too much all the time. With a simpler life, we can take a different view of complications. They are an inevitable part of life, and we have the freedom, flexibility, time and restfulness to take them on as a challenge.

Feelings may come unbidden in the face of complications; they often do. We may be overtaken by excitement or anger, racked with guilt, or brimming with pride. But waiting on the other side of emotion is choice about what we do with the emotion and whatever produced it, what we make from it and build on it. The ability to respond is central to shaping and simplifying our lives.

The next time your simpler life hits a bump in the road or looks like it is ready to unravel, let your emotions have their play. They have their place — they are a vital part of being alive and aware. They help you to know your own heart and mind. But don't let them make your choices for you. Go back to the "I" strands of the simpler life: integrity and intentionality. Let the deeper truths of who you are and what's important to you guide you once again.

Pay attention to whether the complication you face is something that you can change. If it is, then you have the choice to do so or not. If it is not within your power to change the circumstance, then your choice has a different face. It has to do with changing what surrounds the complication, or changing your attitude about it. You still have the ability to respond. Use it in concert with the simpler life you've built.

Carry simplicity within you.

In the final analysis, the question of what we can change and what we can't brings us back to the most fundamental truth of keeping life simple. The simpler life does not ultimately exist outside of us. It exists within.

When we choose a simpler life, we go through a process of overhauling. Along the way, we learn to live on purpose, to let our actions flow out of a heartset that is guided by a "true north," a constellation of values and beliefs. No one has located the human spirit on an anatomy chart, yet neither does anyone deny that it exists. In fact, science increasingly acknowledges the vital part that our spirit plays in our physical well-being, our ability to ride the tides of life and our inclination to make a better world.

If you have chosen a simpler life and want it to continue, simplicity itself needs to become part of your "true north." All the external changes you make to create a simpler life will finally let you down if you haven't created a matching inner life.

A friend recently took a month off, a first in his busy life. He decided to handle this time differently from any of his shorter vacations of the past. His only plan was to let each day happen as it would. No finishing projects, or planning trips or specific events. He promised himself only a genuine rest, a sabbatical from achievement and goals, obligations and hurry.

It was the best vacation he ever took. Why? Because he kept his promise to himself. Every morning, he awoke to an open day and chose what he would do with it. As a result, the vacation took hold *in him*. When he went back to work, he carried the restfulness with him. It didn't happen effortlessly. He consciously continued the same kind of commitment he had exercised during his time off.

Give time daily to recognizing the ways that you are simplifying and the benefits you are deriving. Take moments to be grateful for the good that is growing in your life. Consider future plans or possibilities and test them against your desire to maintain a simpler life. Do they fit? Do they enlarge the character of the life experience you want? Could you do without them? Reflect in this way day after day, and your simpler life will shape the person within. You will carry simplicity with you everywhere you go.

Simpler living is not just an existence trimmed of excess and complication. It is a state of mind and heart, a way of seeing, and a context for doing. As we make simplifying a way of life, we free ourselves to live with more integrity and to act with greater intentionality, which in turn feeds the simplicity. In the process, we gain the freedom and energy to explore new directions, develop the potential in our life and appreciate fully what we already have. We make it possible to extend ourselves for the greater good of others and the world at the same time that we build our personal reserves of joy, satisfaction and courage. And we collect the tools to continue the journey. Life is dynamic. We don't arrive. We are always on the way. That's the journey. Take it gratefully and make it your own.